FORTUNE
Telling

How to Predict Your Personal Destiny

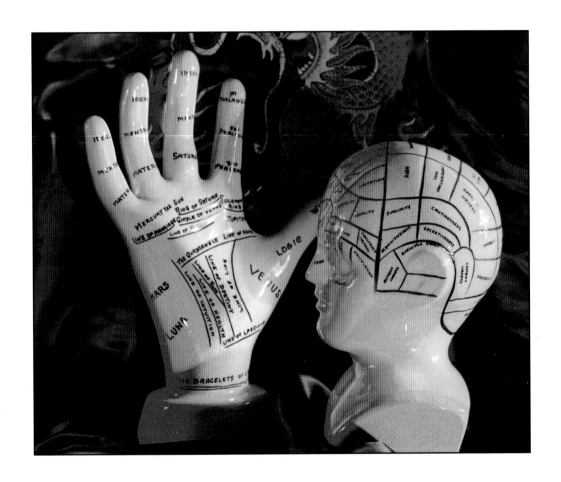

FORTUNE
Telling
How to Predict Your Personal Destiny

BILL ANDERTON

PARRAGON

First Published in Great Britain by
Parragon Books Limited
Units 13-17, Avonbridge Trading Estate
Atlantic Road, Avonmouth, Bristol BS11 9QD
United Kingdom

Designed and produced by
Stonecastle Graphics Limited
Old Chapel Studio, Plain Road
Marden, Tonbridge Kent TN12 9LS
United Kingdom

ISBN 0-75251-719-8

Printed in Italy

Photography Credits:

(*Abbreviations: r = right, l = left, t = top, b = below*)

Images Colour Library Ltd: pages 1, 6, 8, 9t, 9b, 12, 13t, 13b, 14, 16, 17, 18t, 18b, 20, 21, 22, 23 , 24t, 24b, 25, 26, 27, 28, 29, 31, 33, 34t, 34b, 35, 46, 49t, 49b, 57t, 57b, 58l, 59t, 59b, 62, 63t, 63b, 65t, 65b, 66, 67b, 68, 69t, 69b, 70t, 70l, 71, 72t, 72b, 81t, 81b, 82, 83t, 83b, 84.

The Image Bank: pages 2, 3, 10, 11, 19t, 19b, 36, 42, 43, 45l, 47, 50, 51, 52, 53t, 53b, 54, 55t, 55b, 56, 58r, 60, 61, 73, 74, 75, 87, 90, 91.

Telegraph Colour Library: pages 7, 15, 32, 37, 38, 39, 41, 44, 45t, 48, 77, 78, 80, 85, 86, 88t, 88b, 89t, 89b, 92, 93.

Touchstone: pages 40, 67b, 94, 95.

Contents

Omens
from Ancient to Modern Times

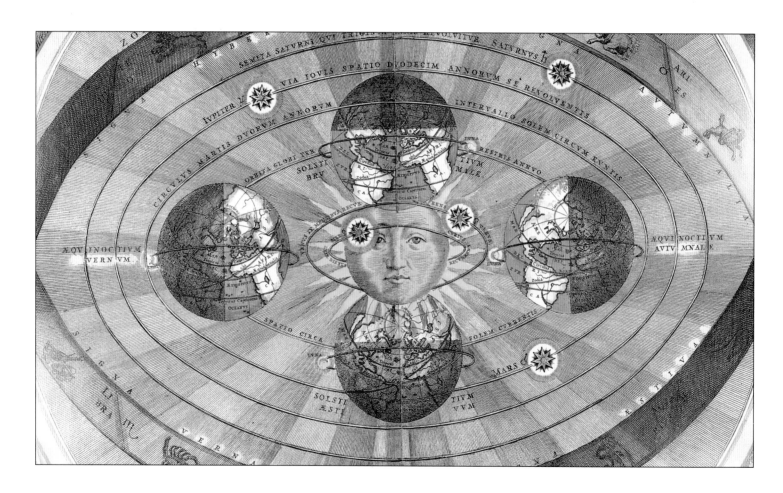

The Copernican system (heliocentric) with the planets and the circle of the zodiac.

Throughout history it has been recorded that there were certain people with an ability to foresee the future and to communicate this to others. The most notable name which springs to mind is that of Nostradamus and his enigmatic predictions, some of which we will consider later.

One reason why we find people like him so interesting is that there is perhaps a 'Nostradamus' in each of us just waiting for the opportunity to exercise his special powers to see into the future.

In this book we are going to explore different methods, or 'oracles', which are employed to achieve this; we are going to examine the whole question of looking into the future – whether or not it is possible and, if it is, how the ability can be learnt and encouraged to develop. First, though, it will be useful and informative to survey briefly the attitudes and abilities that people have demonstrated throughout history and before. Through this you will see that concern for predicting the future is not something new and has a compulsion associated with it that is not just superstition and idle curiosity.

Omens and Signs

Predicting the future can be an exact science when the relationship between a cause and its effect is known. The whole of our modern technologies are built on the ability to predict the outcome of certain events – when water is heated sufficiently, for example, we know that it is going to boil. Boiling can be predicted. This is a simple example, but science is not daunted by more complex ones. The ability to predict future weather patterns is a science, not an exact one because there are so many variables involved, but it is nevertheless a science and one which is based on probabilities, the predicted likelihood of future events.

The patterns and interrelationships of everything that effects the course of events in our lives is so complex that even the power of our scientific world has not been able to turn the art of prediction into an exact science where human behaviour is concerned.

Perhaps one day it will. Despite the complexity of trying to work out the future this has not prevented people in the past from developing their ability to do it. The difference between then and now, however, is that their predictions were not based only on what they observed but what their intuition told them. The similarity was that certain events or 'omens' suggested the occurrence of particular happenings in the future.

Certain Signs Precede Certain Events

It was just as important to ancient people to predict future events as it is today, particularly with our example of the weather. The ability to do this has come down to modern times through superstition and folklore associated with nature. Careful observation of the behaviour patterns of animals, birds and insects reveals information about weather patterns in the future.

This process of associating today's observations with tomorrow's happenings was extended into a whole new field, whereby not only the weather could be predicted but other future events too. The art of predicting the future from signs and omens developed further. Some people seemed to have a natural gift for interpreting the signs. Their abilities eventually became systematized into particular methods of prediction and our legacy today is the various oracles, such as astrology, the tarot, palm reading and so on which we will be examining.

The ability to predict future weather patterns is a science, not an exact one because there are so many variables involved.

Heaven and Earth

A particular example of how certain signs became associated with certain events is in the history of astrology. This first developed in ancient Babylon when the astronomer –priests observed the movement of the planets in the night sky against the backdrop of the fixed stars and their constellations. They developed a system of prediction based on the regular movements of the planets, the sun and the moon. Their records show how particular configurations of the planets would herald either good fortune or impending disaster.

In those times there was little concern to predict the future of individuals, save for that of the current king and how his battles would fare. In other words their concern was for predictions about events that would affect their society and not the individuals in it.

The astronomer–priests laid the foundations of modern astrology, for example describing Mars as the planet of war, Jupiter as a beneficial influence, Saturn as malign, Venus as bringing pleasure and so on. They believed that each of the planets and the sun and moon were living gods who roamed the skies and whose power influenced life on earth.

Collection of shaman's ritual objects, including wooden spirit-helpers, spirit traps, knives, print blocks, human hair purse etc. The objects are from diverse sources, mainly Laotian and Siberian.

Shamans and Shamanism

In all primitive societies, particular individuals seemed destined to develop special powers, powers to heal the sick, powers to solve difficult problems, and powers to predict the future. These individuals would be singled out, and then be subjected to a rigorous and even dangerous training during which time they would be expected to undergo tests and torments, initiating them into the experience of worlds existing beyond that of our own.

If successful, they would assume the mantle of tribal witch doctor, medicine man or shaman, possessing amazing abilities. These numbered the ability to visit other worlds at will and bring back special knowledge to help others, perhaps with a cure for an ailment or with a battle plan, having secured the alliance of friendly gods. Notably, the shaman was able to leave his earthly body and visit other planes, was able to fly freely to other parts of the earth – and was able to visit the future.

Magic, Witches and Warlocks

Every culture has had its shamans and witchdoctors since prehistoric times, but even in our modern age, in the not too distant past, people have expressed a great interest in the possibility of manipulating through magical means the forces of the universe, attempting not only to predict the future but to affect it too. In the Middle Ages there was a great interest in astrology, alchemy and magic.

Alchemy, the forerunner of modern chemistry, attempted to transmute metals into gold and to do this alchemists studied astrology, the relationship between the heavenly bodies, the planets, and experiments in the alchemist's retort – the alchemist needed to predict the future outcome of his experiments.

At the same time many people believed that you could go even further than this and manipulate the creative and destructive forces of the universe, the basis of magic and all its rites, rituals and 'alchemical' potions.

If you wanted a love affair to turn out right, all you needed to do was secure an effective magical potion from the local witch or warlock.

Levitation during a stage-magic act.

Folklore and Superstition

Magic was taken seriously by its practitioners and almost everyone, even today, has a sense that there is at least something in it.

You don't have to delve very deeply to find that there is still a great interest in folklore, and most people have their superstitions, believing that certain acts may bring good or ill fortune.

An example of superstition is that associated with eggs: in a gipsy folktale, a girl noticed that everyone smashed the shell after they had eaten their boiled egg, and asked why. She was told:

You must break the shell to bits for fear,
Lest the witches should make it a boat, my dear.
For over the sea, away from home,
Far by night the witches roam.

I have introduced here the ideas of magic and folklore because the whole subject of predicting the future is commonly associated with them. From out of all this superstition we will be picking and choosing our way carefully to find what there is in it that will be helpful in our quest to predict your future . . .

Dancing devil, witches and toads at a Sabbat. From Dictionnaire Infernale *1863.*

The Mysteries of Time

We may feel unable to break free from the constraints imposed on us by the inexorable passage of time.

To conquer and control the mysteries of time has been a dream for many artists and scientists and still it seems to remain a dream. To be able to move freely backwards or forwards in time is an idea which still exists only in our imaginations.

However, even if we are unable to break free from the constraints imposed on us by the inexorable passage of time, there are some things that can be said about its nature that will help in our quest to reveal the future. In this part of the book therefore, we are to delve into the mysteries of destiny, fate, free will, chance and coincidence.

Destiny, Fate and Free Will

Our culture attaches great importance to the idea of free will – the ability of the individual to choose whatever it is that they would like. This attitude is not the same for all societies and indeed different cultures of the past have put no emphasis at all on the importance of the individual's ability to choose the course of his or her life.

'The freedom to choose' is an ideal; it is obviously not possible, in a practical sense, for it to be available all the time. Our lives are influenced by some factors beyond our control and this is inevitable if we are to live in a society where so much is interdependent. There are forces at work which come together to shape our fate.

What this means is that there will be events in the future which will inevitably happen, which are preordained by the type of person we are, by the circumstances in which we find ourselves. These inevitable, preordained events are what we mean by fate.

The Freedom to Choose

One of the great questions is, can we change our fate, can we indeed affect the future? The answer, I believe, is yes, to the extent that we have free will, have a freedom to choose. But because this is limited, our ability to affect the future is limited too. It is a question of balance and the key is to find out where the balance lies, how much we can affect our futures and how much we must accept the inevitable.

Some people have a strong sense of personal destiny, feeling that they were in some way created to fulfil a particular task in life. To fulfil one's destiny, if you have this sense, is a matter of choice but if you choose to avoid it, then you are going against the stream of life and will find obstacles put in your way. This gives another clue to unravelling the future. We should take into account the possibility of a personal destiny in life.

Our lives are influenced by some factors beyond our control.

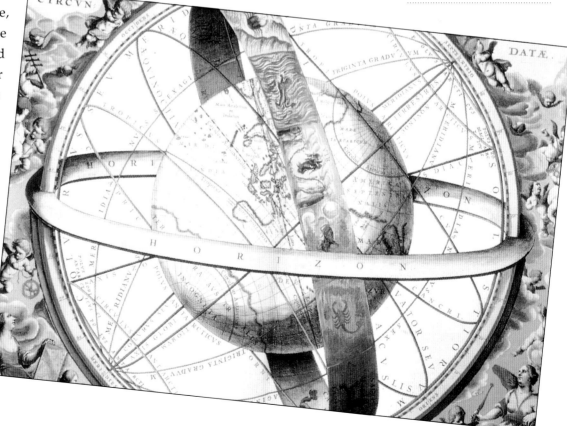

Coincidence and Chance

We have seen how there is a relationship between fate and the freedom to choose. There is another factor to be taken into account when unravelling the properties of time and the future, and this is the nature of chance and coincidence. Some people believe that nothing happens by chance, that everything that happens is preordained, but in the approach that we are taking chance is taken into account.

Life would be extremely dull if it were not for the unexpected, if everything could be predicted according to a mechanical process.

Life is not like that; it has an unpredictable element which has to be taken into account in our predictions. The more we make our plans and try to define exactly what will happen, what course our lives will take, the more likely it becomes that a chance occurrence will interfere in these carefully laid plans and turn them upside down!

Before we consider the different systems for predicting the future, it is important to understand this point. It does not mean that the future becomes unpredictable but it does mean that we should expect the unexpected!

Synchronicity

Coincidence implies that two events have happened at the same time and often a coincidence occurs as if by chance. It is possible to define two different types of coincidence. The first involves pure chance where there seems to be no particular significance in the coincidental events. The second type of coincidence is when the event seems to be full of significance, even if we can't grasp its meaning. For example, you may become interested in predicting the future and then discover that the man who lives next door to you is an astrologer. This may be a chance coincidence but for you it is one that has particular significance. There is a name given to this type of coincidence which was coined by the founder of analytical psychology, Carl Gustav Jung. He described it as 'synchronicity'.

This type of event may seem to the outside world to be meaningless pure chance, but to the person who experiences it, the opposite is true and the event is full of meaning.

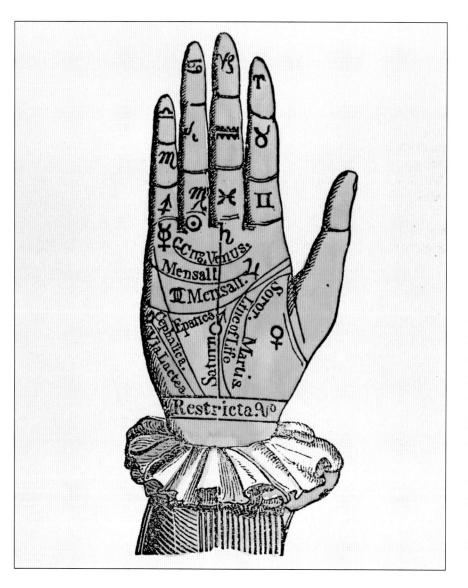

The art of palmistry. Hand marked with main lines, planetary rulers, zodiacal associations etc. From The Imperial-Royal Fortune Teller; and book of Fate, *circa 1860.*

Time & Mysticism

What I have described so far about the nature of time is that although the future cannot be calculated according to fixed laws, it does have certain properties which, when taken into account, illuminate the different systems for foretelling the future which we will be considering. These properties involve the nature of fate, free will, destiny, the freedom to choose, coincidence, chance and syncronicity.

The mystical traditions of different religions also have something to say on these matters and we can learn from them too. Remember that a great number of people in the world believe in reincarnation and that what we have done in past lifetimes affects our destiny in this one. There is a doctrine common to oriental as well as western religions which says that what we sow we will later reap, suggesting that our current

actions not only determine future events but that there is a system of reward and punishment at work too.

Chinese clairvoyant and palmist consulting with client.

Cycles of Life

Both the ideas of reincarnation and reaping in the future what we sow in the present moment suggest the idea of the cyclic nature of time. The symbol of the moon to ancient cultures was a perfect representation of this, the cyclical process being described by its phases. New Moon suggests birth and emergence, Full Moon representing fulfilment and completion.

Each phase of the moon represents a significant time in a cycle of growth, fulfilment, decay, death and rebirth, which endlessly repeats itself. This model of the cyclic nature of time can be applied to anything that comes into existence and then, at a later date 'dies'.

The consequence of this is that life can be viewed as a series of phases and, if we can determine which part of the cycle we are currently going through, then it is possible to make appropriate preparations for the next phase of the cycle, giving another clue to how the process of predicting the future might work.

Personification of the Moon, ruler of Cancer.

The Romany Tradition

A crystal ball may foretell your future. . .

The image of the gypsy fortune teller has been created through a long tradition which still exists today. In this section we are going to look at where this tradition comes from and how it has evolved. Looking into the future, as we have seen, does not only depend on logic and calculation, but a major factor is the use of intuition and even psychic abilities.

Both of these will be considered in detail, but first, what is it that lies in the Romany tradition to give a strong affinity for such mysterious matters? The gypsy fortune teller who can look into your future at a glance may only be treated as a curiosity and a side-show, but there is much that we can learn from their art.

Fortune Telling

I remember having a reading from a gypsy who told me lots of things about myself that simply seemed to be untrue. This puzzled me because the chances of getting absolutely everything wrong are quite low! When I arrived home it occurred to me that what the woman had said was perfectly true, but she had been talking about my next-door neighbour. I learnt an important lesson from this, which I have found valuable ever since. The fortune-teller had been accurate but had picked up facts which were just to one side of their target.

This often happens and seems to be a property of intuitive fortune telling. It is possible to be accurate but just slightly off beam. The message from this is to be careful and to look a little further, if your interpretations do not seem to be accurate. It is well worth looking beyond the immediately obvious.

Fortune telling of this nature is usually purely intuitive or psychic and ones abilities in these areas can play strange tricks, so always be thoughtful and on your guard. Also, remember not to dismiss intuitive information if at first it does not appear to be accurate. It is usually well worth living with it for a while to see what twist or turn might occur.

The Tall, Dark Stranger

So, you are going to meet a tall, dark stranger, come into money and have all the things you have always dreamed of. So says the fortune teller. Now, were you hearing the things that you wanted to hear? The answer is probably yes and this is an important point to learn when looking into your own or anyone else's future. Out of all the information that we are presented with, it is quite normal for a person to be selective and only hear what they want to hear.

This adds difficulty to a reading because not only are we being presented with information which is not yet tangible and therefore sparks ones imagination in all sorts of directions, but we are also unconsciously choosing and picking what we want to hear and what 'seems right' for us.

The gypsy fortune teller knows all about this – and so must you if you are to practise the art – for predicting the future is not only a matter of divination but of accurate communication too.

The gypsy fortune teller who can look into your future at a glance may only be treated as a curiosity and a side-show, but there is much that we can learn from their art.

Reading the Cards

One of the tools commonly used for predicting the future is an ordinary set of playing cards. We will examine in detail the Tarot cards which have much in common with modern playing cards, and it is well worth noting that playing cards can be used in exactly the same way as the Tarot – spreads being created with individual cards each interpreted with their own specific meaning.

Playing cards and the Tarot deck each have four suits with cards numbered from one to ten, each having court cards associated with the suits. The two main differences are that the Major Arcana of the tarot (see page 31) has disappeared from the deck of playing cards. Also, the Tarot is often pictorial, whereas playing cards, apart from the court cards, are always based simply on numbers.

I like using playing cards because the meanings associated with each card are clearly defined. The tradition of fortune telling from playing cards has almost disappeared in comparison with the current popularity of the Tarot, but I can recommend their use. They are well worth investigating and can provide much accurate information.

This formal pattern is designed to reveal the issues relating to a question concerning the future. The card at the top of the cosmic cross (directed to Cancer) relates to career.

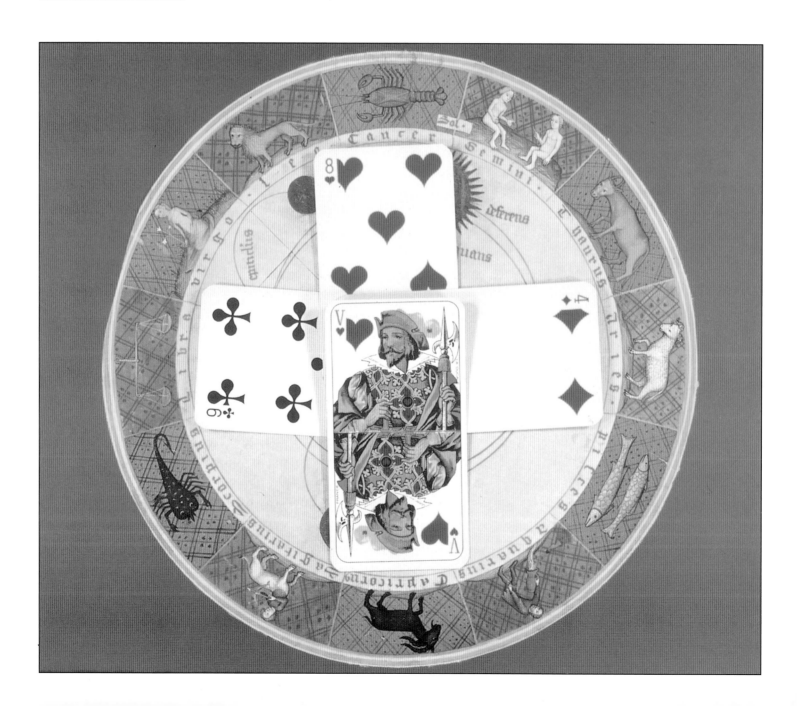

Mademoiselle Lenormand

Born on 27 May, 1792, in Alençon, France, Mademoiselle Lenormand is known and acclaimed as a great clairvoyant. Her reputation is based on her oracular deck of playing cards which she probably designed herself and which carries her name today.

In Paris she opened a salon for the upper levels of Parisian society and here she used the cards, astrology and other divination techniques to predict the future for her clients. Powerful and wealthy Parisians vied for the chance to visit the 'Sybil of Faubourg

Saint Germain' in her salon in the rue de Tournon. Her astonishingly accurate predictions of the future and the fates of individual questioners caused her fame to increase not only in France but in other countries as well.

The clairvoyant predicted that Josephine and her husband Napoleon would one day ascend the throne of France. It is reported that Napoleon laughed out loud when he heard about her prediction. History proved her correct.

The Lenormand Oracle

There are 36 cards in the Lenormand oracle. The cards are numbered from 1 to 36, each has a picture and a title and a specific meaning, and each is associated with a card from the normal playing-card deck. For example, the first four cards are as follows:

Card No.1, the Cavalier represents News (Nine of Hearts)

Card No.2, the Clover represents Hope (Six of Diamonds)

Card No.3, the Ship represents Journeying (Ten of Spades)

Card No.4, the House, represents Hearth and Home (King of Hearts)

And so on. When you have determined exactly what question you wish to ask the oracle and the cards have been properly shuffled, a spread is made and the cards interpreted according to their individual meanings. As we shall see with the Tarot, the cards are not only interpreted individually but their relative positions in the spread and their relationships are taken into account too.

The Art of Crystal Gazing

Although crystal gazing is one of the best known forms of divination, it is also one of the most difficult to practise. The purpose of crystal gazing is to produce images in the crystal itself, not in the mind. Some argue that these images actually appear within the gazer's mind, but most practitioners disagree. While the crystal may, indeed, stimulate psychic awareness, the ball itself creates the images. The awakened psychic awareness is of use simply to assist in the interpretation of the responses received.

This is why crystal gazing requires a seer of a sensitive and receptive nature. Though you don't need to be psychic, it helps. 'Crystallomancy' is best performed at night, ideally on the full moon or during its waxing. Lower the lights but leave a single candle burning and sit with your back to this light source, ask your question and then wait for the images to appear. Gaze into the sphere, not at its outer surface or at any reflections from the room that may be visible. Let yourself go.

Rock crystal ball on tripod stand – the caryatids representing the three Fates.

Palmistry

This is another favourite for the gypsy fortune teller and everyone knows the significance of their life line, even if you don't know exactly where to look for it. Palmistry is possibly the oldest form of character reading, first appearing in Chinese history more than two thousand years ago. Although it is the lines on our hands which show many things about our characters, our health, our mental and emotional natures, relationships, talents and longings, palmistry is the study of the hand in its entirety, not just the lines and marks on its surface.

Above: Johann Hartlieb first published a book about palmistry in 1460.

Below: Modern palmists make great use of palm-prints which may be enlarged to show minute detail.

You will find in the study of palmistry that there are many links with astrology as many astrological terms are used. I hope to show in this book how all the different methods for predicting the future have common strands which we will use to develop a simple and unique system for foretelling your future.

Astrology and palmistry have been linked for many centuries. Each finger is associated with a planet. It was once thought that the planets influenced the make-up of the hands to correspond with the influence that they had on forming our personalities and our destiny.

Tarot Predictions

We will spend some time examining the Tarot cards and how they are used for making predictions but this is an appropriate place to introduce them as they form an important tool in the Romany tradition of fortune telling. No-one really knows where the Tarot cards were originally developed or how they came into being, but one thing is for sure that they have a long and mysterious history.

The Tarot cards are not simply a set of cards, each with an individual meaning, but, like palmistry, contain links with other branches that we will cover such as astrology and numerology, the study of number symbolism.

There are 78 cards in a Tarot pack, 22 in the Major Arcana, 16 court cards and 40 numbered cards, 10 in each of four suits. The court cards and the numbered cards make up the Minor Arcana, which has a direct relationship with our modern deck of playing cards. Only one of the Major Arcana cards has survived the transition to the 52-card deck, the Fool surviving as the Joker.

The Psychic Gift

Everything in our lives is interconnected, even if the connections are not visible or immediately obvious. Our everyday awareness only represents a small part of all the possibilities that are presented to us both from outside by our senses and from inside from the unconscious.

Sometimes we receive unbidden hunches or intuitions and for some people these can be very strong, taking the form of perhaps images or thoughts which seem to come from nowhere. Such sensitives are said to be psychic and it is possible to train this sensitivity both to heighten it and to learn how to interpret the experience. In the Romany tradition the psychic 'gift' has appeared often and with many people.

This gift, to receive and interpret impressions connected with the questioner's past, present and future, can be used in conjunction with any oracular method of fortune telling, whether it be palmistry, crystallography, or Tarot reading.

My experience has shown me that it is not necessarily a special gift though; psychic abilities lie dormant in everyone. If you are drawn to this area, perhaps through psychic experiences of your own, then I will describe how to develop this ability on page 42.

Psychometry

Try this. Take an object which belongs to another person, ideally someone with whom you have an acquaintance but do not know intimately. The object could be a brooch, a watch, a pen, anything that the person owns and has around them during the day.

Hold the object in your hand and close your eyes. Imagine that the object creates impressions in you, sends you messages that enter your mind. These impressions may come in the form of pictures, images, sounds, even smells, or simply thoughts or feelings.

Spend some time opening yourself up to these impressions and let them come. When you have finished, write

the impressions down and begin to think about what they might mean, where they have come from and what they are trying to tell you. Then you can talk about it with the object's owner.

You may surprise yourself that you have been able to find out things about the person you did not know but were conveyed to you through contact with the object.

This is the art of 'psychometry' and there are overlaps here with psychic awareness, enhanced by the use of a particular object, imprinted with its owner's 'vibrations'.

Sometimes we receive unbidden hunches or intuitions . . . taking the form of perhaps images or thoughts which seem to come from nowhere.

Spend some time opening yourself up to these impressions and let them come.

A Trip Around the Astrologer's Universe

A German broadsheet, from circa 1540, depicting a giant comet terrifying the people as it swoops over a mediaeval city.

A strology is the study of the relationship between the stars and planets and our lives on earth. Astrology was once taken very seriously and the greatest minds and philosophers devoted much effort to it. Since the middle ages the popularity of astrology has declined except in magazine-type horoscopes which everyone finds irresistible.

There is a more serious side to astrology, however, which involves the interpretation of the horoscope, or 'birth chart' and it is this which we will examine in this section. Astrology is based on the idea of cycles and patterns in life, which correspond with the cycles of the planets. Not only is it possible to analyse these cycles in the past and present but they give a clue to the future too.

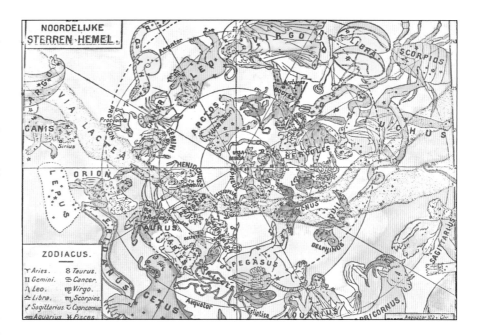

How Astrology Works

The astrologer's main tool is the birth chart. This is a map of the heavens drawn up for the time, place and date of birth of the individual to whom it will refer. It shows the positions of all the planets in the signs of the zodiac at the time of birth.

The skill of the astrologer is to interpret the birth chart, which is said to set the pattern for the growth of the person throughout their life. In other words, what will happen is described by the positions of the planets and the signs of the zodiac at birth. Astrology is based on a system of 'correspondences', which means that each planet, for example, corresponds with different ways of behaving, different personality patterns.

Astrology appears to be complicated because of all the calculations that are necessary to set up a birth chart. In fact when you learn astrology you will find this is not true. The calculations are quite straightforward. Computer software is also readily available to take all the hard work out of it.

The Horoscope or 'Birth Chart'

Your birth chart is a map of the heavens, showing the signs of the zodiac and the planets, as seen from your place of birth. This is why astrologers need to know your time, date and place of birth, to draw up an accurate chart.

This is usually drawn in the form of a circle, with the signs of the zodiac displayed around the outside of the circle. The main constituents of the birth chart are: the signs of the zodiac; the houses; the planets; and the aspects.

The signs of the zodiac represent twelve personality types, influencing the planets that are placed in them.

The astrological houses, of which there are also twelve, represent twelve different areas of life.

The planets, the sun and the moon, represent different parts of an individual's personality.

The aspects show the relationships between planetary energies and how these planets will affect you.

To modern astrologers, the birth chart is a cosmic mirror – when you look into it you see yourself, not, of course, your physical features, but those of your personality, your natural abilities, your inner tensions, and your potential for the future.

A hand-coloured constellational chart from Aq. Libra's 'Astrology – its Techniques and Ethics', one of the earliest astrological studies to introduce New Age concepts.

Signs of the Zodiac

Each sign of the zodiac represents a personality type:

Aries is pioneering and an energetic leader.

Taurus is down to earth, consistent, productive and forceful.

Gemini is fickle, light-hearted and versatile, with a quick mind.

Cancer is sensitive to emotions, receptive to the needs of others and protective.

Leo is the play actor, and can play a role to the hilt, provided admiration is forthcoming from his audience.

Virgo is self-sacrificing and adopts the role of giving service to others.

Libra is the diplomat, seeking justice and looking after everyone's interests.

Scorpio is concerned with hidden depths, with what lies beneath surface appearances.

Sagittarius is the optimist, open to new experiences to adventure and travel.

Capricorn is the empire builder, ambitious, paternal and authoritative.

Aquarius is humanitarian, is the eccentric, the visionary and the inventor.

Pisces is a peace lover and dreamer with an impressionable and active imagination.

Left: Leo, the lion.

Below: Virgo, the virgin.

Above: Aries, the ram.

Right: Taurus, the bull.

Planets

Right: Libra, the scales.

Each of the planets represents a particular human attribute:

The sun represents the will to live and gives a sense of purpose.

The moon represents feelings and emotions.

Mercury represents intelligence, mental capacity and communication.

Venus represents the ability to form relationships, to fall in love.

Mars represents energy, drive and aggression.

Jupiter represents the urge to grow and expand ones horizons.

Saturn represents limitations and discipline.

Uranus represents the ability for invention and innovation.

Neptune represents the ability to imagine and gives a sense of the mystical in life.

Pluto represents the power to regenerate.

Even without your birth chart you should be able to say which of the above planets have most influence in your life and which seem to play a role of lesser significance. Incidentally, astrologers count the sun and moon as planets because they appear to move around the earth even if this is not the case.

Above: Gemini, the twins.

Right: Cancer, the crab.

Astrological Houses

Your birth chart is divided into twelve areas called the 'houses' and each of these areas represents an area of your life:

House 1 is the house of your self-image, the role that you adopt in life.

House 2 is the house of material possessions.

House 3 is the house of communications and sibling relationships.

House 4 is the house of home, childhood and roots.

House 5 is the house of creativity and children.

House 6 is the house of health and the capacity to work.

House 7 is the house of partnerships.

House 8 is the house of death and birth, and of other people's resources.

House 9 is the house of education, philosophy, religion and travel.

House 10 is the house of vocation and social achievement.

House 11 is the house of groups and societies, also ideals and aspirations.

House 12 is the house of the unconscious, of things 'locked away'.

Left: Scorpio, the scorpion.

Below: Sagittarius, the archer.

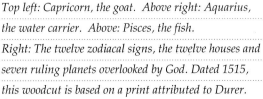

Top left: Capricorn, the goat. Above right: Aquarius, the water carrier. Above: Pisces, the fish.

Right: The twelve zodiacal signs, the twelve houses and seven ruling planets overlooked by God. Dated 1515, this woodcut is based on a print attributed to Dürer.

Personification of the Sun, from an alchemical plate in the 'Mutus Liber' in the Jacobus edition of 1702.

Woodcut of Hecate, the Moon Goddess, with her dog and serpents, and crescent moon on her forehead. 17th century.

The Sun

Of all the planets, the sun and moon are the most important. When you tell someone what your birth sign is you are telling them the sign of the zodiac in which the sun was positioned at the time of your birth. The sun has a lot to do with the development of personality. It represents the process of self-development, whereby a person becomes whole and fulfilled. It symbolizes the life force and therefore the true Self, the centre of personality. It is a masculine, outpouring energy, the energy of life, and influences ones sense of purpose.

The sun regulates and maintains equilibrium, so if there is a sense of imbalance in your life, it is the sun that needs to be looked at in your birth chart. The sun also has much to do with strength of will – the ability to achieve your ambitions and desires. Positively expressed, the sun is self-assured, independent and creative; negatively, the sun expresses egotism, incompetence and aggression.

The Moon

The moon is a symbol in your birth chart representing emotions, feelings and the unconscious. The main purpose of the moon is to give form and substance to the life force. The sun provides the initial impulse, but it is the moon that makes this impulse fertile and gives it material expression. The moon is a reflective feminine archetype, whose function is to respond, to nurture and to give form. Astrologically often associated with the mother, the moon in your birth chart also symbolizes the past, memories and childhood.

The moon contributes to emotional sensitivity and the way we respond to experiences, both outer and inner. Strong likes, dislikes and prejudices are attributed to the moon. Its constructive qualities are sensitivity, sympathy, protection and affection. Its negative qualities are moodiness, unreliability, being wilfully destructive and easily influenced.

Your Rising Sign

When your chart has been drawn up, it will show the sign of the zodiac which was rising over the eastern horizon at the time of your birth. This is called the 'Rising Sign' or 'Ascendant' and has a special significance. The Rising Sign is closely associated with the first house, which, if you remember, is the house of your self-image.

The Rising Sign represents the role that you adopt in life, the image that you like to project to others and the way that you would like other people to see you. This is different from your true inner self, which is represented by the sun and the sign in which it is positioned. Outwardly a person can appear to be very different than when they are at home or in private. The outer skin or 'persona' is what the Rising Sign represents.

In addition, the Rising Sign is ruled by a particular planet and this too, astrologically speaking, has an important influence. For example, if, say, you have Gemini Rising in your chart, then as Gemini is ruled by Mercury, this planet is said to be your ruling planet. The part of your personality which corresponds with Mercury will, in this case, be prominent. As you can see from the above information about the planets, Mercury represents intelligence, mental capacity and communication skills.

Astrological Aspects

When two or more planets form a particular relationship with one another in your birth chart, they are said to form an 'aspect'. The aspects are shown in the centre of the chart as a criss-cross pattern of lines joining the planets involved. These are referred to as the aspect lines. When an aspect occurs, the qualities of two planets (or more) are linked together. Some of the aspects are interpreted as difficult ones, when the planets do not get on, so to speak. These are tensions, sources of conflict and, if resolved, sources of growth and creativity for the individual.

Other aspects are interpreted as easy or flowing, in which case the two planets operate well together, and they are interpreted as natural abilities.

The aspects link the planetary energies together and represent the way that inner relationships are formed between different parts of your self, between your 'head' and your 'heart', for example.

Interpretation – How It's Done

So far I have described the constituent parts of the birth chart. How are these parts drawn together and an interpretation made? Like most divination systems, the interpretation needs to rely on the astrologer's intuition to determine which parts of the chart stand out and seem important and which can be ignored. Interpretation of a birth chart can also be learnt and the way this is done is usually in the form of keywords.

For example, a keyword for Mercury is 'communication' and a keyword for Venus is 'relationships'. If Mercury and Venus form an aspect in a chart that is positive, then we could say that communication and relationships work well together, meaning that this person finds it easy to communicate within their relationships. If badly aspected the opposite could be true.

Keywords for the signs of the zodiac and the houses are also taken into account to give more depth to the interpretation. For example, if Venus was in the tenth house, then relationships would be focused on career and achievement.

Quite a detailed interpretation can be built up using this method, which is quite easy to do as long as you know the keyword meanings for the signs of the zodiac, planets, houses and aspects.

The Moon and its influence over zodiacal signs and over people.
From the Bib. Estrense *(Modena) edition of 'The Sphaera'. 15th century.*

Predicting the Future

People often accept that a birth chart can identify particular personality traits but do not understand how free will or experience can be incorporated. A man of 50 may well have similarities with his five-year-old self, but will hopefully have learned to modify and develop various attributes. At 50, however, he still has the same birth chart as when he was born.

The movement of the planets can account for these changes. They are always on the move and their patterns of interrelationships (the aspects) continuously change too.

The position of any planet at any time can be compared with its original position in the birth chart. These new 'transiting' aspects are interpreted in exactly the same way as the aspects shown within the birth chart. The main difference is that they can be interpreted to suggest future trends.

Once this idea has been grasped, of how the movement of the planets can be related to the birth chart, it is possible to take into account the cycles of each planet. These are determined by the length of time it takes for each of them to make a complete orbit. Saturn, for example, takes about 28 years to complete an orbit, and 28 years is recognized by astrologers as a particularly significant cycle in the life of an individual.

Mars, Jupiter and Saturn.

Patterns & Cycles

If you consider the birth chart as the starting point, the planets each have an unfolding pattern which repeats every time a cycle or orbit is completed. The approximate cycles associated with each planet are as follows:

Sun, 1 year   **Jupiter**, 12 years
Moon, 28 days   **Saturn**, 29 years
Mercury, 1 year   **Uranus**, 84 years
Venus, 1 year   **Neptune**, 164 years
Mars, 2.5 years   **Pluto**, 248 years

Saturn is a particularly important planet from this point of view. It will have completed its cycle at about 29 years old, and again at about 58 years during your life. Astrologers interpret each of the stages during these cycles. It is worth mentioning that the time of life associated with the 'Saturn Return' at the end of the 20s and again at the end of the 50s can be particularly testing times, bringing personal crises that can be turned into opportunities.

The planets Mercury, Mars, Venus, Sun and Moon inset within zodiacal band. From about 1612.

Learning Astrology

Astrology is a fascinating subject partly because there is so much that can be learnt about it. However, for our purposes it is only necessary to learn the basics, which I will use later in the book as part of a unique system for predicting the future. If you want to avoid one time-consuming part of astrology, namely calculating and setting up your birth chart, it is easily possible to obtain one from an astrologer or even to buy a computer programme which will do the job for you.

The process of learning about astrology is first to learn what the birth chart is, how it is built up and what it contains. In learning about this you will be finding out about the symbolism of the planets, signs of the zodiac, astrological houses and the aspects, just as they have been described above.

Once you have discovered the key to interpreting your own chart you will be able to apply the method to any chart. Try to be methodical in your learning, at least at first, for there is much information about traditional astrology that you need to know before you can begin to explore the new possibilities opened up by astrologers of our own time.

Psychological Astrology

Many astrologers say that the birth chart sets an underlying pattern for the individual's life. It seems to me that the value of the birth chart can become more acceptable by taking this a step further and saying that it simply forms a mirror into which you can look to see yourself. What you see is a reflection of your personality, of drives and inhibitions, talents and weaknesses. It will reflect both unconscious and conscious aspects of yourself. Also, as we saw earlier, what you see in it is what you choose to see.

The birth chart encapsulates the quality of a particular moment in time at a particular place – at your birth – but beyond this it acts only as a tool, providing an opportunity to reflect the whole person, inner and outer, past and future.

It is significant that the birth chart is drawn up for the time of birth, for this is a symbolic act making this cosmic mirror personal to the individual. But the main point is that it does become nothing more than a passive mirror – there is no need to talk about mysterious beams emanating from Jupiter or Venus, controlling our futures!

The twelve signs of the zodiac from a late 15th century manuscript.

Tarot Cards for Fortune Telling & Fun

Reading the Tarot. The formal pattern is set out in the traditional Tarocchi design and there are several other decks on the table.

More than any other system for fortune telling the Tarot cards carry an aura of mystery about them. There is no doubt that their history is a long one, going back so far in time that it is impossible to be certain about their origin. One thing is certain, however, and that is the popularity of Tarot divination, witnessed by the great number of different decks which are available today.

Some of these decks are quite old in their design and many of them are modern, the artwork and symbols depicted on them being inspired by many diverse ideas. Whatever the name on a deck, whether it be The Medicine Woman Tarot, The Enchanted Tarot, or Tarot of the Cat People, the method for reading the cards is the same and it is this method which we will now explore.

The Tarot Story

The invention of the Tarot cards has been attributed to various sources. Some have seen in the word 'tarot' a corruption of the name Thoth, the ancient Egyptian god of magic, reinforcing the legend that the cards were created in the initiation temples of the mysterious East. Their invention has also been attributed to the Order of the Knights Templar, an ascetic military Order founded in 1188 to protect pilgrims and guard the routes to the Holy Land.

Whatever the rumours about their appearance, the tarot is closely linked with our modern deck of playing cards. It is generally accepted by scholars that the earliest playing cards originated in China and Korea, dating back at least to the 11th century.

If Tarot cards, as seems most likely, were devized originally somewhere in Northern Italy, it can be surmized that their makers were perhaps inspired by oriental cards brought from the east by merchants returning to the great trading port of Venice. The original 78-card Tarot pack is generally referred to in Italy as the Venetian or Piedmontese Pack, to differentiate it from later offshoots.

Tarot Techniques

The basic idea in using the tarot is that the cards are shuffled and a 'spread' created. This means taking cards in sequence from the top of the shuffled pile and placing them in a particular pattern with the cards face up. The position of a card in the spread will signify a particular subject, such as the past or future of the person consulting the cards, the 'querent', and a specific card thus positioned will be interpreted according to its meaning.

You will see from this that, having posed a question to the Tarot deck which the querent requires to be answered, the cards chosen and placed in the spread appear simply by chance, as the pack is first shuffled. It is 'fate' or 'chance' which determines which card appears in which position.

Before making the spread, the cards are shuffled in such a way that some cards will appear upside down and others the right way up. A card that appears upside down, or 'reversed', has a different meaning than if it had appeared the right way.

Each card has a particular interpretation but it is not quite as straightforward as this as the relationships that appear between different cards in a spread should be taken into account too.

Recreation of a 16th century pack, after the so-called Cary-Yale/Visconti pack.

How the Tarot is Structured

There are 78 cards in the deck, which is divided into two parts: the Major Arcana or Trumps, and the Minor Arcana. The word 'arcana' means mysteries or secrets. The Minor Arcana consists of 56 cards divided into four suits, each suit having ten Pip cards and four Court cards. Apart from the extra Court card in each suit (the Knight), the Minor Arcana resembles a pack of modern playing cards, but the suits have different names:

Wands, Rods or Batons (corresponding to Clubs); Cups (corresponding to Hearts); Swords (corresponding to Spades); and Coins, Pentacles or Discs (corresponding to Diamonds).

Court cards are usually called King, Queen, Knight and Page.

The 22 cards of the Major Arcana form a sequence of 21 numbered cards, plus one unnumbered card called the Fool, which is sometimes numbered zero. Each of the Major Arcana cards depicts a strange scene which appears to have allegorical significance, telling a story or conveying a message. Each card is appropriately titled – the Sun, the Lovers, the Tower, the Hanged Man, Justice, the Emperor, the Star, the Chariot, to name a few.

There is a specific order to the Major Arcana cards, but some decks deviate from this. The cards of Justice and Strength are most commonly transposed, this occurring, for example, in the popular Rider-Waite Tarot deck.

How a Spread is Made

The illustration shows a typical spread, this one called the Celtic Cross, or Ten-Card Spread. The cards are laid out in order, with the following meanings:

Card 1: Questioner's Present Position

Card 2: Immediate Influence on the Questioner

Card 3: Questioner's Goal or Destiny

Card 4: Influences Coming from the Distant Past

Card 5: Influences Coming from Recent Events

Card 6: Influences Coming into Being in the Near Future

Card 7: Questioner's present position or attitude

Card 8: Questioner's Influence on Other People and Vice Versa

Card 9: Questioner's Inner Emotions, Hopes and Fears

Card 10: Final Results – The Outcome

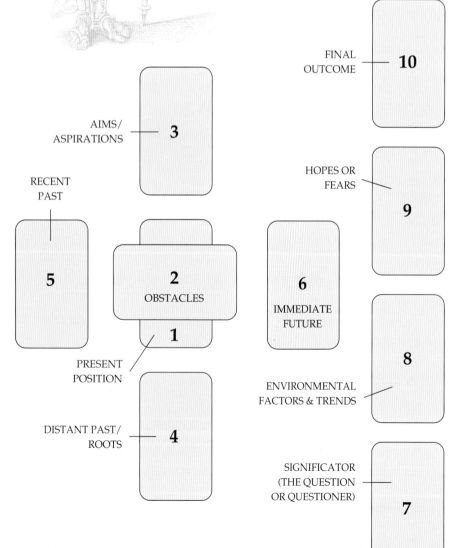

The Major Arcana

It seems likely that the Tarot cards, and in particular the Major Arcana were devised to represent grades or stages in a system of initiation. It is possible to interpret the meanings of the cards in terms of a sequence of events or lessons to be learnt. There seem to be close links with the system of alchemy whose devotees believed in the Hermetic philosophy and underwent training leading to spiritual enlightenment.

These ancient doctrines have been examined afresh in modern times, particularly by C. G. Jung, who described the alchemists' work in terms of what he called 'psychic integration' or 'individuation'. The Major Arcana in this light becomes more than just a tool for divination but a way of learning about ones inner self and deeper motivations.

If we examine the 22 Tarot trumps with this in mind, we find that they fall naturally into two groups, with the Wheel of Fortune significantly at the midpoint. The turning point between one half of life and the other is of critical importance, sometimes precipitating a mid-life crisis. In this context the Wheel of Fortune represents the stage at which the peak is passed and the descent begins.

A selection of cards from the Major Arcana in different designs.

The Minor Arcana: Cups and Wands

The Minor Arcana is divided into four suits: Wands, Swords, Cups and Pentacles. Each suit corresponds to one of the four astrological elements, Fire, Air, Water and Earth.

The suit of Cups corresponds to the element of Water. The Cup represents our ability to contain and to manage our feelings and emotions. Hence the suit of Cups is associated with feelings and emotions – the cup can be empty or full, it can be of great concern or ignored, its contents can be poison or elixir. The liquid contained by the cup symbolizes the sea of the unconscious, the source of all life, the most liquid, changeable formless and yet most powerful force in our world. As the Holy Grail, the cup can be a cornucopia, supplying all our wishes in a never-ending supply.

The suit of Wands corresponds to the element of Fire. Fire is a creative force which can illumine and warm, or, if uncontrolled, will burn up and destroy. Wands represent the creative urge, the imagination and the will to bring ones dreams into reality. This suit has much to do with dominion and the establishment of power through strength, strife and victory. Its negative connotations being of oppression and the misuse of power.

The Minor Arcana: Pentacles and Swords

The suit of Pentacles corresponds to the element of Earth. Its realm is that of the material world, our possessions, our material successes and losses, whether we are prudent and thrifty or wasteful, whether we will have wealth or suffer poverty. This suit also represents earthly power and the ability to make practical changes in our lives.

The suit of swords is a very active suit often suggesting conflict and strife.

The suit of Swords corresponds to the element of Air. It has much to do with the way we think, the things we believe to be true or not. It is also a very active suit often suggesting conflict and strife and the outcome of our battles to earn success. Sorrow and despair can be found in these cards as well as attainment and happiness.

Here is a summary of each card in the four suits:

Cups: 1 Water; 2 Love; 3 Abundance; 4 Blended Pleasure; 5 Loss in Pleasure; 6 Pleasure; 7 Illusionary Success; 8 Abandoned Success; 9 Material Happiness; 10 Perpetual Success.

Wands: 1 Fire; 2 Dominion 3 Established Strength; 4 Perfected Work; 5 Strife; 6 Victory; 7 Valour; 8 Swiftness; 9 Great Strength; 10 Oppression.

Pentacles: 1 Earth; 2 Harmonious Change; 3 Material Works; 4 Earthly Power; 5 Material Trouble; 6 Material Success; 7 Success Unfulfilled; 8 Prudence; 9 Material Gain; 10 Wealth.

Swords: 1 Air; 2 Peace Restored; 3 Sorrow; 4 Rest from Strife; 5 Defeat; 6 Earned Success; 7 Unstable Effort; 8 Shortened Force; 9 Despair and Cruelty; 10 Ruin.

The Court Cards

In a Tarot reading, the Court cards are generally thought to represent particular individuals – either the querent, people known to the querent, or people he or she will meet.

The Court cards are part of the Minor Arcana and therefore are associated with the suits. The elements associated with the suits affect the personalities of the characters depicted. The Court cards in the suit of Wands are influenced by the element of Fire, which makes them lively and extroverted, while the Court cards in the suit of Cups are under the influence of the element of Water, which makes the characters they represent quiet, introverted and inclined to daydream.

The Court cards in the Air suit of Swords represent intellectual people who depend upon rational thinking, while the Court cards of the Earth suit of Pentacles are practical, common-sense people, good with their hands, skilled at making things work or at least with the potential to do so.

Number Symbolism

Not only are the pictures on the Tarot cards representative of their meanings, but the number of each card is too. Later, we will examine the idea of divination from the meaning of numbers, but specifically in relation to the Tarot deck, the number association of each card, whether Major or Minor Arcana is as follows:

Zero: Latent potential
One: Wholeness and unity
Two: Relationship, duality
Three: Creation, resolution
Four: Wholeness, stability
Five: Instability, hazard and struggle
Six: Harmony, balance and equilibrium
Seven: Wisdom, fate, supernatural powers
Eight: Material success and justice
Nine: Achieving results
Ten: Completion and the beginning of a new phase.

Links With Astrology

Apart from the association of the four suits with the four astrological elements, astrological symbolism abounds in the Tarot. Images such as the lion in the Strength card obviously correlate with the sign Leo; the Chariot with lunar crescents evokes the sign Cancer; similarly the lunar images of the High Priestess mark her as a goddess of the moon; the association of the Death card with the sign Scorpio is clear; the garden couch of the Empress is decorated with a Venus symbol, clearly evoking Venus; the Tower is destroyed by a burst of energy which is of the planet Mars; and the Sun card literally corresponds to the astrological symbolism of the sun.

These and many other associations have been made between the astrological symbols of the zodiac and the planets and the images found on the Tarot cards. This is useful in helping to bring new dimensions of meaning to the cards and also demonstrates quite clearly that the systems of divination that we are covering have much in common – when you learn about one system you are learning about the others too. The common factors will be of great help to us in developing a new oracle and we are now one step further on the way to doing just this.

The Tarot cards associated with the zodiacal constellations on an old star map.

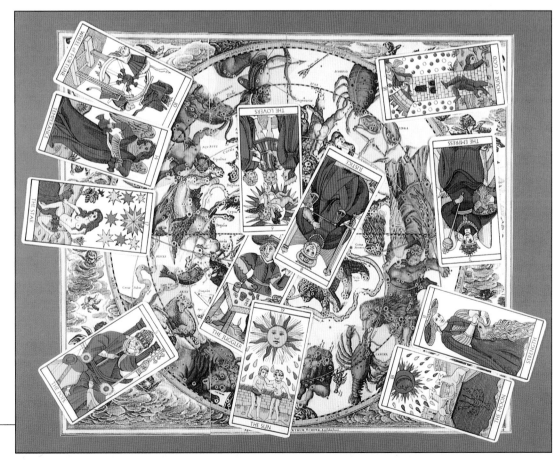

Card Symbols

Girl reading the Tarot.
The pack is the Oswald Wirth
design.

We have seen how the number associated with a card can give a clue to its meaning, and so too can the images which are found on the cards. Some of these symbols can be found on more than one card and it is worth exploring their meanings. Here are some of them:

Pairs of columns symbolize the physical world and its vested authorities.

Stars and canopies symbolize the higher worlds available through increased awareness.

The throne is dominion, power, strength and fixity.

The pyramid is transmutation to reach a higher reality.

The Square and **Triangle** are the same in interpretation to the numbers four and three, described above.

The Sphere represents completion.

Towers symbolize strength and protection.

The Crown symbolizes high status.

The Sceptre symbolizes fertility.

Keys are the means for unlocking a problem.

An Arrow represents the strength of willpower.

A Snake suggests wisdom.

Corn is a symbol for renewal and harvest.

Roses symbolize love.

Trees symbolize strength, union and the linking of heaven and earth.

The dog is loyalty, instinct and faithfulness.

Cats suggest intuition and perception.

Mountains symbolize a quest and the scaling of great heights.

A Barren Landscape represents lack of love and affection.

There are, of course, many other symbols to be found on the cards. The point here is that it is worth not only learning about the meaning of the cards, but also about the individual symbols which are included in each illustration.

Tarot reading using the
traditional Marseilles deck.

Choosing Your Deck

Your choice of Tarot deck should be guided by your own intuition and aesthetic sense. The vital factor is that the images on the cards should be ones with which you can identify and which inspire you.

It is best to avoid cards with 'cartoon style' images which tend towards superficiality. Cards with too much ornate design also tend to distract from their essential meaning. Go to a shop which stocks several different decks and examine them until you find one that you feel comfortable with.

My likes and dislikes will not be the same as yours but as a rough guide I can recommend as a first pack any of the following: The Rider-Waite Deck; The Aquarian Tarot; The Prediction Tarot; The Morgan-Greer Tarot; and the Hanson Roberts deck.

If you are feeling a little more adventurous, try The Golden Dawn Tarot or the Crowley-Thoth Deck.

Two modern decks which are a little bit off the beaten track but are nevertheless well worth exploring are the Enchanted Tarot and the Mythic Tarot decks.

Some decks will appeal to people with quite specific interests, like the Medicine Woman Tarot, or the Tarot of the Cat People.

Getting Started

Having obtained your Tarot deck, my suggestion is to try a reading straight away, perhaps using the Celtic Cross spread which I described. There is nothing like learning by doing and no matter how much you learn the meanings of the individual cards you will find that the essence of the Tarot does not reveal itself until you actually use it in a reading.

Be quite clear about the question that you wish to ask. This is a general rule relevant to any divination system. A question whose meaning and motives are vague or ill-defined will result in an answer that is also unclear. However, this does not mean that you cannot ask general questions. For example, you, or the person for whom you are doing a reading, may simply wish to have a reading that summarizes your current situation and describes where exactly it is leading. You may be confused about a particular issue in your life, or uncertain about the correct decision to make. The Tarot will help to clarify your circumstances.

Another general piece of divination advice which can be applied to the Tarot is to resist asking the same question twice. This applies particularly if you don't like the answer that the reading gives. Also, the same question should not be asked within a short period of time, otherwise the answers will be conflicting and confusing. The rule is to wait until your circumstances have made a definite change before consulting the Tarot again on the same issue.

Working With Your Tarot Cards

As a final thought in this section it is worth knowing that the Tarot cards can be used in other ways than as a tool for predicting the future. I suggested that the Major Arcana tells a story representing the search for and the achievement of spiritual enlightenment and that a modern interpretation of this process is to do with seeking and finding ones personal needs in order to become fulfilled and whole.

Try living with each of the Major Arcana Cards in turn, perhaps in their number order, or perhaps in the order that they appear after shuffling, contemplating their meaning and the relevance of the individual card to you. You could even try meditating on the card's image and see what ideas spring to your mind in association with it.

Not only will this process of 'working with the cards' throw new light on the meaning of them, but the process will work in reverse too, the cards throwing their meaning back to you, giving you insights into your own deeper, unconscious nature, suggesting things that you need, things that you should do in order to grow and develop into a complete and fulfilled individual.

Girl in gypsy costume reading the Tarot cards. This deck is said to have been designed by the great modern Spanish artist Salvador Dali.

The Secrets of Numbers

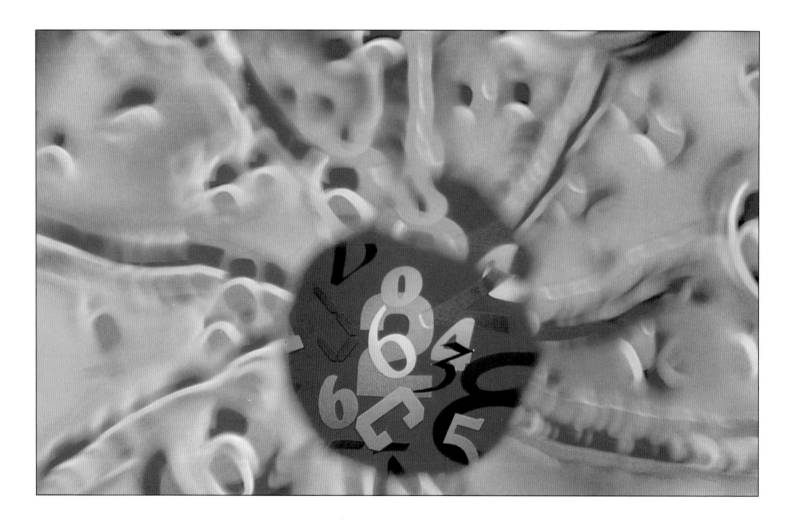

To ancient mathematicians numbers were not simply numbers, they had a mystical, separate reality of their own.

Investigating the different methods of divination makes it clear that there are common threads that run between them all. We have seen, for example, how the Tarot and astrology have much in common. The most useful theme which links different oracular systems is that of Numerology, the study of number symbolism. In this section we are going to delve into the secrets of numbers.

This will help us in our quest for developing a unified system for predicting the future and help to explain each system that we examine. Numerology is also a potent divination system in its own right. In this section you will learn the meaning of numbers and how to work out your own personal numbers, the number of your name, your personal birth date number and the pattern of your destiny.

The Art and Science of Numerology

Modern scientists and mathematicians would certainly not subscribe to the idea that numbers have individual personalities, that they have a life of their own and that they are creative forces. But this is precisely what the mathematicians of old believed and it is their legacy that has developed into the modern practice of Numerology.

To these ancient mathematicians numbers were not simply numbers, were more than ideas; they had a mystical, separate reality of their own. So, in developing their mathematics they also looked at the quality of each number, at its personality and began to record what they found. Their belief was that the numbers in your life appear by plan and by providence. Behind each and every number there exists specific potentials that can profoundly influence and affect your personal growth and development. The art and science of numbers were not separate and making calculations involved working with living entities. So what are the personalities that these first mathematicians discovered in numbers?

Numbers As Symbols

Numbers have personalities that suggest particular potentials, influences and possibilities, and you have a relationship with them. Each and every number in your life is a symbol for a highly charged potency of energy. The symbolism associated with your personal birthdate number and your personal year number, for example, has a connection and relationship with you that makes you what you are, and what you will become.

The character of your numbers inspires the character of your life, your personality and experiences being influenced by the properties and potentials of the numbers that live in you.

A symbol has depth. It is not just one-dimensional, it reveals different facets as you explore it. It can even change with time as new meaning unfolds from it. Symbols can be described as having a life of their own and this accords with the ancients' description of numbers as living entities. Our personalities are complex and so too are the things that influence us and create our futures. Symbols, such as numbers, are a useful way of encapsulating that complexity and making it simple. Numbers are the essence of our selves. When we explore them they start off as seeds and then flourish and grow as we begin to discover their meaning and see ourselves in them.

The symbolism associated with your personal birthdate number and your personal year number, for example, has a connection and relationship with you that makes you what you are, and what you will become.

Pythagoras's Ideas About Life, the Universe and Everything

This is how Pythagoras, the Father of Mathematics, described the dawn of creation:

From the monad came the indeterminate duad; from them came numbers; from numbers, points; from points, lines; from lines, superfices; from superfices, solids; from these, solid bodies, whose elements are four: *viz.*, fire, water, air, earth; all of which, under various transmutations, the world consists.

The philosophers of ancient Greece, such as Pythagoras, were among the first to attribute a great and precise sanctity to numbers, particularly the first ten integers.

Numbers were thought to be symbols for the building bricks and the fabric of creation. They represented the archetypes through which the unmanifest could manifest. A study of numbers was considered, therefore, to be a study of God and of God's Creation, a truly sacred science.

Numbers were thought to be symbols for the building bricks and the fabric of creation.

Interpreting Numbers

Zero: The number of the future, containing all things that will come into being, and to which they will return, the number of potential.

One: The number of unity, of beginnings, the first signs of something coming into being, traditionally associated with the physical body.

Two: The number of duality, contrast, tuned to emotion, empathy, intuition, instinct and caring.

Three: The number of balance and resolution, linked with thought and the mental processes.

Four: The number of solidity and stability, empowering the will, determination, endeavour and discipline.

Five: The number of human creativity, promoting versatility and originality, encouraging change and variety.

Six: The number of profundity, insight, and knowing, encouraging the pursuit of wisdom, the number of the sixth-sense.

Seven: The number of contemplation, meditation and deep thought, activating awareness of spiritual dimensions.

Eight: The number of networks and organization, the fundamental number which holds everything together.

Nine: The number of the power of the law and of completion, promoting truth and judgement.

Numbers and Your Personality

Before beginning to explain the basics of a numerological reading, I want to emphasize the relationship between numbers, personality and the future. The key to this understanding is that, although there are some simple basic formulae for working out the numbers associated with you, there is nothing in numerology to suggest that preparing a reading is a mechanical process of calculation followed by looking up the meaning of the individual numbers.

Numerology is in exactly the same category as other oracles whereby there is a certain structure and blueprint that can be created, but thereafter, the interpretation allows for the fact that the numbers are symbols. They should be treated according to the description of the ancient philosophers as having a life of their own and therefore not fixed in their meanings which will change, grow and develop.

We will meet this again when considering the interpretation of dreams, whereby the text-book meaning is only a starting point, an anchor which keeps our interpretations anchored in reality. Don't be put off by the apparently cold, defined nature of numbers.

When you start to experiment with them you will bring them to life. You will find that they have the ability to make connections, with you, with your past and with your future.

Your Name Has a Number

One of the most potent shapers of our personality, and therefore a shaper of our personal future too, is our name. Our name seems to hold all the qualities of who and what we are. Numerologically, there is a direct link between the prime numbers and the letters of the alphabet, so that it is possible to analyze our personal name in terms of number.

Pythagoras created the Pythagorian Chart to identify the numbers behind names, the chart aligning the letters of the alphabet to one of the primary nine integers:

1	2	3	4	5	6	7	8	9
A	B	C	D	E	F	G	H	I
J	K	L	M	N	O	P	Q	R
S	T	U	V	W	X	Y	Z	

To discover your name number, first assign each of the letters in your full name to a number according to the above table. L, for example, is assigned the number 3. Next add all of the letters of your first name together to arrive at a single number, repeating this for all of your names. Add them all together and then reduce to a single, final number as in the example below:

F R E D	**S M I T H**
6 + 9 + 5 + 4	1 + 4 + 9 + 2 + 8
= **24**	= **24**
= 2 + 4 = **6**	= 2 + 4 = **6**
6 + 6 = **12** = 1 + 2 = **3**	

The end point and final name number is reached when the numbers have been reduced down in this way to a single digit, in this case the number 3. This is the number to which this name and personality is attuned. Try it for your own name.

One of the most potent shapers of our personality, and therefore a shaper of our personal future too, is our name.

Your Personal Date Number

Exactly the same principle can be applied to discovering the number which is associated with your birth date, a number which, like your astrological birth chart, is a seed from which everything that you are, grows.

For example, if you were born on 8 December 1949, first ascribe a number to the month. December is the 12th month of the year and therefore is ruled by the number 12. The pattern is thus: 8 (day) 12 (month) 1949 (year).

Now apply the numerological method for number reduction to find the single number that represents this date.

8	12	1949
8	1 + 2	1 + 9 + 4 + 9 = 23
8	3	2 + 3
		5

$$8 + 3 + 5 = 16 = 1 + 6 = \mathbf{7}$$

The number that rules this date is the number 7. Try it for you own birth date.

. . . a number which, like your astrological birth chart, is a seed from which everything that you are, grows.

The Pattern of Destiny

Having determined the number vibration which accords with your birth date, it is possible now to take the process one stage further by considering the quality of any year in your life simply by determining the number associated with that year. Discover the number, know its meaning and you have a key to unlocking the future.

Here's an example. For the person whose birth date is given above, what would be the key description for the year 2000? Take the birth date, but this time replace the birth year by the year in question:

8	12	2000
8	1 + 2	2 + 0 + 0 + 0
8	3	2
8 + 3 + 2 = 13	1 + 3 = **4**	

The number governing the year 2000 for this person is the number 4, and from our knowledge of its meaning we can say that this will be, for them, a year of great stability, productivity and material gain. Try it for yourself, for any year that you choose. You can try it for the past as well as the future to see how accurate it is.

The Numerological Year

To make the reading even more specific, it is possible to apply numerology to a particular year, as already described, then to a month, and hone the reading down to a particular day.

To arrive at your personal month number, you simply add your personal year number to the number of the particular month you would like to investigate, reduce the number down to obtain a single digit and this is the number for the month in question.

If there was a particular day in this month that you would like to know about, then the procedure is as follows. To arrive at your personal day number, add the personal month number that you have just found to the calendar day number. Once again reduce the result numerologically to give a single digit, and this is your personal day number.

In this way you can predict the quality, according to the number symbolism, of any day at all, no matter how far in the distant future, or even just a week ahead. Try it for yourself.

Number Predictions

Numerology, as I have described it above, is first of all a process of reduction. The qualities, the essence, the influences, all the complicated factors that go to make up the events of a moment in time are reduced to the number that describes them.

The next part of the process is almost the opposite. The number you have obtained is taken as the basis of an interpretation, first equating the number with its traditional meaning and then expanding on this using your intuition as well as your knowledge about number symbolism.

The process of expanding on the meaning of the number is exactly the same as it would be if you were considering a Tarot card, or interpreting an astrological birth chart. First define the meaning according to the archetypal interpretation of the number, but then begin to make free associations. I choose the word 'association' carefully here because I am not suggesting that you simply let your imagination roam free and make the interpretation depend on whatever pops into your head. Association means that you are making connections to the anchor of the number symbol.

Expanding on the interpretation, whether using Numerology or any other divination system, is helped by the development of intuitive and even psychic powers, and it is this that we will explore in the next section.

The complicated factors that go to make up the events of a moment in time are reduced to the number that describes them.

Inside the
Psychic Mind

Even if you don't feel you possess great psychic powers it is an ability that lies in all of us and can be drawn out and developed.

So far we have been examining oracular systems for foretelling the future, so that the main feature for prediction has been that of following certain rules and guidelines to make the system work for you. In each case, however, it becomes apparent that there is more to making an oracle work than simply following its rules and calculations.

There is a 'factor X' at work too which I have described as intuition, free association and psychic awareness. It is the latter that we are to investigate now. Even if you don't feel you possess great psychic powers it is an ability that lies in all of us and can be drawn out and developed, if you wish to do so.

Psychic Powers

It is difficult to define exactly what psychic powers are, or what a psychic experience is, because the experience is a personal one, it is subjective – it cannot be measured in any way. The simplest way to describe it is as a sixth sense, a way of experiencing other than through our five physical senses. The experience itself is nothing extraordinary, psychic sensations coming in the form of thoughts, feelings, images, sensations even smells. But the interpretation of where these come from is different.

Psychic abilities were particularly associated with spiritualism and contacts made by the psychic with those who were deceased. This association still exists today but is not what we are concerned with here. By psychic experiences I mean inner knowledge and awareness that come from external events, situations, circumstances, in a way other than through the physical senses. It is a sixth sense experience.

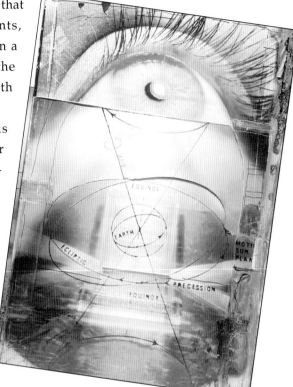

Working on the basis that everything in our universe is connected – including our relationship with the future – and that this sixth sense is a reality, it follows that it is possible to use it to penetrate beyond the veil of everyday reality to see into the future.

How to Develop Psychic Abilities

In this field it is a good idea to have a teacher, someone who knows what to expect, what the problems are and how you can best develop. This is not always possible, so here are some suggestions.

To make an oracle work effectively for you it is necessary to use intuition and even psychic powers. You will find that the opposite is true too, that by simply using an oracle and becoming familiar with it, you will begin to develop your psychic insights naturally. Simply be aware of what is happening and encourage the experience appropriately.

Another key which I have found particularly useful is meditation, which I will be describing more fully. Meditation encourages a state of relaxed awareness, the ability to watch and observe ones inner experiences, to allow them to grow and develop. Then you can interpret these experiences and begin to understand where they have come from and what they are trying to say to you.

Don't be afraid of developing your psychic abilities for they are completely natural, but you must exercise some common sense here. For example, if you have an overactive imagination, then developing psychic powers is the last thing that you need. Quite simply, if it feels OK, then fine, if not, then don't do it.

Don't be afraid of developing your psychic abilities for they are completely natural.

Natural or Supernatural?

Psychic awareness is often thought of as the result of supernatural powers at work but in my experience this is not the case. It is a perfectly natural experience and can be compared with musical ability. Some people have special talent which comes quickly and easily, others can develop their talent but have to work harder at it. We all have an innate musicality even if we never use it or seek to develop it. Psychic powers are just like this.

It is possible that this sixth sense has died away through lack of use. There is a belief that ancient peoples had a natural psychic ability and sense, which in the course of recent evolution has disappeared, because its importance has gradually been diminished. There is even an 'organ' in the brain that is associated with the psychic sense, known as the third eye, situated at the front of the brain and associated with the pineal gland.

In Hindu scriptures, the third eye is associated with a particular centre of consciousness or 'chakra' called the 'ajna' centre. This Sanskrit word is translated as 'to know', 'to perceive', or 'to command', giving further clues as to the purpose and identity of this centre. It suggests a sort of psychic command centre.

There is even an 'organ' in the brain that is associated with the psychic sense, known as the third eye, situated at the front of the brain.

How to Use Psychic Power

Remember the section that we covered on psychometry (see page 19)? Using your psychic powers is just like this. It is the ability to open yourself to impressions which come from within but which are associated with some outer object. In the case of psychometry it is quite literally an outer object. In psychic awareness the object can become anything that you like, a person, a situation, the future.

Try this. Work out your personal day number for tomorrow, as described in the previous chapter on Numerology. When you have worked out the number, meditate on it. See it in your mind's eye and open yourself to impressions, in just the same way that you did in the earlier psychometry exercise. What thoughts, images, ideas, feelings arise in you in response to the number? Accept whatever comes to you no matter what and when you have finished your psychic meditation, write down what you experienced.

Keep your notes until the day after tomorrow and then look at them again. Even though your impressions may not have made sense at the time, you may surprise yourself at the insights that you obtained.

Intuitions

Although the experience of intuition is not the same as psychic awareness, it does have much in common with it and is therefore worth considering. A useful definition of intuition is being able to see future possibilities. An intuitive type of person does just this. Give such a person an idea and they will immediately start thinking in terms of its potential. Perhaps thinking is the wrong word to use here as intuitions are not thought out but are instantaneous. They are rather like going straight to an answer without having to go through the process of working it out.

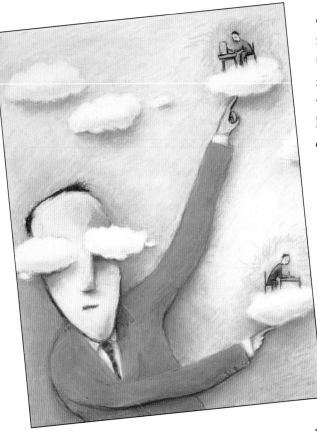

Successful business people are usually intuitive types being able to grasp possibilities, see potential, glimpse future outcomes and then act accordingly on these insights. It is quite clearly not as simple as this though. How does one know whether or not an intuition is true, is the right path to follow?

The answer to this is that intuitions should not be followed in isolation. In other words simply acting on an intuition without any other thought is not a good thing to do. An intuition may come spontaneously, but acting on it needs to come after consideration, after thinking it through. The same is true of psychic experiences. They need putting in a context and thinking through.

Clairvoyance

A common form of psychic experience is that of clairvoyance. A clairvoyant's psychic sense talks to them in terms of pictures. There are other forms of psychic sense – clairaudience means receiving thoughts and words rather than images; clairsentience means receiving feelings and sensations. All these are equally valid, but I have singled out clairvoyance as it has special qualities. Because the experience comes in terms of images, the process – and its interpretation – has much in common with understanding precognition in dreams, which will be considered in the next chapter.

Developing clairvoyance is a creative process involving the encouragement of ones imagination, rather like daydreaming but in a controlled and purposeful way. In modern psychologies this ability is described as active imagination or guided imagery. The images are not interpreted literally but are treated as symbols, in just the same way that we have been considering the symbols of astrology, or those found on the Tarot cards.

This is generally true but not entirely. Some psychic experiences can be direct and literal. The trick is in learning what should be accepted as straightforward information and what should be interpreted as symbolic, as representational. This ability comes with experience.

Developing clairvoyance is a creative process involving the encouragement of ones imagination, rather like daydreaming but in a controlled and purposeful way.

Successful business people are usually intuitive types being able to grasp possibilities, see potential, glimpse future outcomes and then act accordingly on these insights.

Psychism

There are many different facets to the psychic experience. Our concern here is with seeing into the future, but other aspects are worth considering to give a full picture of what psychism is all about. Some of these will be considered in the following sections, but it is important before continuing to emphasize that psychic experiences should be treated with some caution.

To develop and exercise ones psychic powers to greatest effect requires above all, honesty. It is all too tempting to make great claims which no-one can dispute because the experience is an inner one. When you communicate psychic insights, no-one will be able to dispute their validity because only you will have had the experience.

An appropriate tale which can teach us here is that of *The Emperor's New Clothes*. Remember the invisible clothes which actually were not there, but nobody dared to admit this because of the Emperor's authority! Don't play the emperor but be as honest as you can with other people and particularly with yourself.

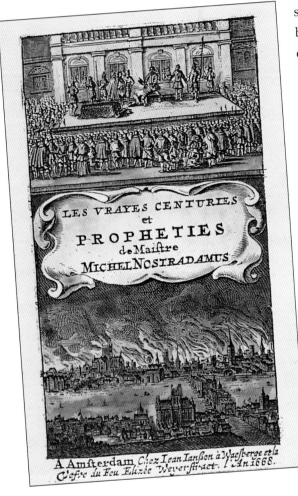

The title page of the 1668 edition of the Prophecies *(Centuries) of Michel Nostradamus, printed in Amsterdam.The illustrations point to two notable prophecies within the centuries – the execution of King Charles in London, and the Great Fire of London.*

Looking into the Future

Here's another exercise for you to try. As in the practice of psychometry, choose an object to hold or touch. It could be anything in your possession but I would suggest something old, that has a history going back further than you can remember. Let's say that you choose an old trinket box that was given to you by a grandparent.

Touch your object and run your fingers over it, feel its weight and receive as much information as you can about its size, shape and texture. Think about its use; begin to think about its history, who might have made it, where it might have lived before coming to you. Begin to be fanciful, using your imagination about its history, about what might have happened to it, about what course of events led up to it being in your possession.

Close your eyes and allow these impressions to continue. Now imagine that it is some time in the future. See the object in your mind's eye and again allow impressions to come to you. Open yourself to whatever your unconscious will allow you to see.

This is a good exercise for developing psychic insight, for it begins with the measurable, with the objective, then shifts your perception into the realm of memory and the past, and finally moves it in the direction of the future. The exercise is a series of connected stages and types of awareness, each leading to the next and finally leading into the psychic dimension. Try it.

Meditation

I have already mentioned the value of meditation in developing psychic awareness, and the exercise you have just done leads into a meditation on the object you chose to take you into the future. So what is meditation? In this context, it has little to do with the classic notion of emptying your mind. Rather the opposite is true. You are opening your mind, aiming for a state of receptivity to whatever impressions crop up.

To be effective, this type of meditation needs to be a state of relaxed awareness. To achieve this, it is necessary first to relax. You will find that your intuition and your psychic impressions come much more easily when you are in a state of relaxation.

A simple technique to achieve this is first by concentrating on your breathing, which should be slightly deeper than normal and evenly controlled. Secondly, become aware of each part of your body in turn and relax it, and finally, you can increase your relaxation by saying a phrase to yourself, such as 'I am becoming completely relaxed and open to whatever experiences come to me'. Try it.

Just a few minutes practising meditation each day can bring great benefits, not least in creating the sort of consciousness within which your psychic experiences can flourish.

Psychic Healing

In developing your psychic powers you will become aware of your healing powers too. Not only will you be able to receive psychic impressions of your needs and those of others, but will become aware of what should be done to improve your state of health. It is quite common for someone to develop psychic abilities and find that they have the power to heal too. You may find that changes in your diet or your lifestyle become appropriate for you.

In encouraging psychic powers, you are dealing with a state of awareness that penetrates beyond the everyday, and forges a link between our normal awareness and that which lies beyond the surface. The key here is of forging a link, of making a relationship between two regions of awareness which are usually unrelated. This itself is a process of healing, of making whole.

In this holistic world, where all things are connected, as soon as you forge this link, then healing power is released. In terms of predicting the future, you will develop the ability to see where a problem might lie and what its future solution should be. Even more than this, you may find that you carry the means for making other people whole or healed as well as yourself.

The development of psychic powers has consequences that lie far beyond the original spiritualist conception of communication with the deceased.

In this context, meditation has little to do with the classic notion of emptying your mind. Rather the opposite is true.

Seeing the Human Aura

Some psychics claim to see what they describe as an aura of light around the human form. What they describe is an envelope of coloured light emanating from the human body, surrounding it and protecting it. Rather like crystal gazing, seeing this aura may not come easily, for, although it depends on an inner openness and awareness, the aura itself does not exist in the mind but is seen actually surrounding a person.

To clairvoyant vision the aura betrays the habits, attitudes and potential of each person. The generous person has an expansive, softly coloured aura; the miser's is murky and contracted; the aura of a sensual person is crimson whereas that of the materialist is orange. The normal aura radiates to a distance of about a metre, showing colouring that is sometimes radiant, sometimes murky, depending on mood and state of health.

If you are using an oracle to predict the future for someone other than yourself, take the condition of their aura into account when doing the reading. The practice of seeing and reading auras will help you to develop your psychic powers, leading to a greater ability to make the oracle work for you and reveal its future secrets.

If you are using an oracle to predict the future for someone other than yourself, take the condition of their aura into account when doing the reading.

Energy Centres of the Body

The centre of awareness associated with the sixth sense, is the ajna chakra, or third eye. In fact, seven different chakras have been identified, each of them being centres of different types of awareness or consciousness. More about the chakras can be found in the ancient Hindu religious texts called the *Upanishads*, which indicate their locations in the body and give symbolic descriptions of their properties.

Pictures, images, birds, animals, gods and goddesses are used to describe their qualities, giving a feel for what the chakras are all about. Correspondences in the western interpretation of the chakras include different colours, giving a link with the paragraph above on the colours of the human aura.

The seven chakras and the colours associated with them are: the base centre, red; the sacral centre, orange; the solar plexus centre, yellow; the heart centre, green; the throat centre, blue; the brow centre (third eye), indigo; the crown centre, violet.

Interpreting Visions

Particularly when we come to the interpretation of prophetic dreams in the next chapter, you will see how important it is to adopt the right approach to interpretation. Interpreting your psychic experiences, interpreting dreams, and interpreting the information that you see in your oracle are all facets of the same jewel. You may look from a different direction when considering each one, but whichever direction you look from, you are looking at the same thing, the jewel itself.

The interpretation process is the same in each case. First, accept whatever comes to you without question and without censorship. Simply observe and take careful note. The next stage is to expand the experience by making associations, by thinking about it and by talking about it. In doing this you can use your knowledge about symbols or about the particular oracle that you are using. The next stage is to allow your psychic impressions time. Live with them for a while – don't simply interpret them on the spot then forget about them. You will find that once they have been born, they need time to grow and develop. In time, you will come to have new insights and make new realizations about their meaning.

To be psychic, you need to be sensitive to all possibilities. Don't impose limits on yourself and your abilities. Where the future is concerned, there are always new avenues to explore.

Psychic Protection

Experienced psychics know the value of psychic protection, for in developing your psychic awareness you are opening yourself to receive all sorts of impressions to which your sensitivity is increased.

A simple protection exercise is to visualize a cross within a circle. The circle is a universal symbol of healing and wholeness. Picture the cross within the circle radiating light energy that fills you and radiates out from you, creating a protective aura or shield.

Each time you exercise your psychic powers, do this little exercise both at the beginning and at the end as an act of protection.

And now, having delved into the realm of the psychic we can turn to another source of inner visions of the future, namely prophetic dreams.

The vision of the Apocalyptic Woman, from the Apocalypse series Apocalypsis cum figuris *of Albrecht Durer, 1498.*

The vision of the Whore of Babylon, from the Apocalypse series Apocalypsis cum figuris *of Albrecht Durer, 1498.*

Dreams of the Future

The way that we communicate with the unconscious is through our imagination, through our thoughts and feelings, and, in sleep, through our dreams.

It has become clear in our exploration of future predictions that the approach has taken two directions. First, we are considering different oracles, how they are set up and interpreted. In addition, we have been considering the nature of time, the future, and our relationship with it. This has meant delving into the workings of the mind, the unconscious and, in the last chapter, the role of intuition and psychic perceptions.

Continuing this theme, we are now to consider the role played by our dreams, particularly those which seem to point to happenings in the future. Even if you cannot claim to have had a psychic experience, everyone has experienced what it is to dream and has touched on the mysterious power which lies behind them.

Letters from the Unconscious

The unconscious is like another person inside us which contains everything other than our everyday awareness and perceptions. It is the source of all our creative powers, it holds our memories and extends beyond our personal experience into what Jung called the collective unconscious. This suggests that there is a factor of the mind which is common to all of us. The way that we communicate with the unconscious is through our imagination, through our thoughts and feelings, and, in sleep, through our dreams.

Dreams are letters from the unconscious, their messages are couched in symbolic forms, and here you can see an immediate and important link with everything that we have touched on so far. The language of dreams and that of the oracle for predicting the future, both talk in symbols, usually in the form of images or 'imaginations'.

Of interest to us here are those dreams that are prophetic and give us glimpses of the future, but the whole subject of dream interpretation is directly relevant in teaching us more about the nature of symbols and how to read them.

Encourage Your Dreams

Do not despair if you cannot remember your dreams! Try some positive thinking. If you suggest to your unconscious that you cannot remember your dreams, then it will respond accordingly. Try suggesting to yourself that you can remember your dreams and await the response.

The technique is to go to sleep at night with the thought in your mind that you will remember a significant dream and, remarkably, you will find that you will be able to. You can encourage the process by keeping a pen and paper close to your bed so that you can write down your experience as soon as you wake, for, as you know, the memory of dreams can fade quickly as the images slip back into your unconscious.

This technique of self-suggestion can be taken further by suggesting to yourself that you are going to dream about a particular situation or receive an answer to a specific problem. You can even suggest that your dream will be about the future.

Here is the key to this process: treat your dreams as if you were consulting an oracle. As we have done before, make your question as clear as possible, so that the answer from your dream will be equally clear. Don't force the process. You may need to wait for several nights before an answer comes, before a dream occurs. An oracle has a mind of its own when it is brought to life by consulting it. Treat your dreams with respect, be open to them and they will come to you.

Treat your dreams with respect, be open to them and they will come to you.

Dream Symbols

Images in your dreams can have two dimensions to them. The first dimension is 'collective' or 'archetypal'. This means that the meaning of the symbol is a universal one, the type of meaning that you can read in a dream dictionary. For example, a snake appearing in a dream can mean wisdom or renewal. These are archetypal interpretations of the symbol which we can all agree on, and which has been the meaning of the symbol since the time of early cultures.

Our personal feelings and associations have to be taken into account when interpreting a dream symbol.

Each image has another dimension to it, namely the 'personal' dimension. This means that a symbol, such as a snake, will mean different things to different people. We will each have our personal associations to make. For example, one person may feel good about snakes, whereas another might find them repulsive. Our personal feelings and associations have to be taken into account when interpreting a symbol, whether it be that of a dream, or indeed of a symbol presented by any of the oracles that we are considering.

This makes interpretation more interesting. It means that no-one can fully interpret your dream for you, no matter how expert; only you can bring the personal dimension to bear. A knowledge of the archetypal meaning is useful but not the whole story.

Dream Interpretation

A dream interpretation can be done in two parts. First, make a note of the different images that appear in your dream, a sort of dream inventory. Then find out what the archetypal significance of these symbols might be. You will find that a good dream dictionary is useful at this stage (see page 94). Then, in addition to these interpretations, add your own comments describing how you feel about each symbol, and any other associations that you can make as well. At this stage don't try to see how the different symbols relate to one another, but simply examine them individually.

The second stage is to explore the relationships that exist between the symbols in your dream. Are there any common linking factors, threads of any sort linking them together that might suggest a common theme? Consider the overall feeling of the dream and try to sum it up in one or two keywords or phrases.

It is at this stage that you may well come to realize what the specific message of your dream was. Note again that this process of dream interpretation could be applied to any oracle, so you can see that we are beginning to treat dreams in a way that fits in with our approach to discovering the future.

Prophetic Dreams

Prophetic dreams have been reported throughout history, occurring particularly when momentous events are about to take place. Such a dream might occur to you but is unlikely. What is likely, however, is that you may experience dreams, particularly if you encourage them in the way already described, that bring messages to you about your own future.

A prophetic dream will occur when the unconscious has something to say to you of importance for your own future health and well-being. One purpose of dreams seems to be to encourage balance when an unhealthy imbalance has occurred in life. Perhaps you are working too hard and your dream could show you what the outcome will be if you continue. The aim of the dream is to show you the necessity of relieving stress before you damage your health. The unconscious has your interests at heart in maintaining a balanced life.

In this instance the prophetic dream's purpose is to change the future, to warn of a future negative outcome which can be avoided. There are also dreams which predict inevitable events too. The unconscious can look into the future. A possible reason for this is that the unconscious – and therefore

dreams – is not bound by the laws of our everyday universe, and in particular is not bound by the limitations of the time dimension. We cannot move backwards and forwards in time, but our dreams seem to have no difficulty in achieving this.

Warning Dreams

Those dreams that seem to have most effect on us and which seem to carry most power, are those which have come through from the unconscious to achieve an important purpose. One such purpose is to restore balance to our lives, another could be to warn of impending disaster.

It is well recorded how people have dreamt about natural disasters, only to read in the news the next day that such an event actually happened. Warnings of aeroplane crashes are common in dreams, for example, but should we take them seriously? The answer is yes, but with a qualification. Remember that dreams speak in a symbolic language and almost all the time the messages that they convey are for us, for the dreamer, and not for other people. So, a warning dream might suggest impending disaster and the first place we should look in order to avert it is in our own lives. Dreaming of an aeroplane crash happening in a foreign country does not mean that the dream has nothing to do with you. Neither does it mean that such a disaster will happen – although it could.

If a dream contains an element of warning, then look straight away at what is going on in your own life and what might be looming in the future that the dream tells you to avoid.

A warning dream might suggest impending disaster and the first place we should look in order to avert it is in our own lives.

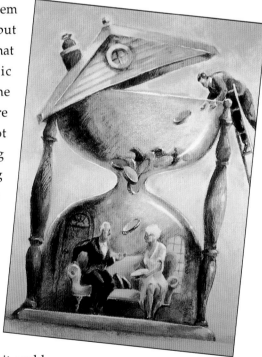

You may experience dreams that bring messages to you about your own future.

Lucid Dreaming

Research is continuing at present into the phenomenon of lucid dreaming. This strange state of consciousness occurs when the dreamer seems to be able to make conscious decisions from within the dream experience. This means that the dreamer finds him or herself in a dream but can then determine how to proceed – the lucid dream is characterized by the ability to make and act on decisions consciously taken.

The experience of a lucid dream can be quite exhilarating. The dreamer might find it possible, for example, to breathe under water or to fly, and then experience directly what the sensations produced by these activities are like.

The composer Wagner is known to have had lucid dreams. In one, recorded by his wife, he found himself in a hall full of classical busts which could speak. Attracted to a particular female bust, he said to himself, 'I do not wish to dream that I kissed her, because it is not good to kiss dead people in your dreams.

Everything in a dream should be taken as representing something about yourself.

The possibilities of lucid dreaming are only just being realized. Perhaps the direct experience of travelling forward in time into the future is not so far fetched any more.

Analysing Your Dreams

We have already described one approach to dream analysis which involves considering the archetypal and then the personal nature of dream symbols. I have also touched on another important point which is worth considering further. Everything in a dream should be taken as representing something about yourself, even if you dream about another person who you know. It is possible to have a dream which is not about you, but this is not generally the case.

When interpreting a dream, consider everything as if it were a facet of your own personality. If you dream of your neighbour and this person is characterized by being bad tempered and unfriendly then it is most likely that your dream is presenting to you a part of yourself which is bad tempered and unfriendly.

Sharing a dream is an effective way of interpretation. In discussing it with someone else, who may be able to point things out that you hadn't thought of, you will be making associations and seeing yourself in what is said, and therefore seeing yourself in the dream. This is the main point here, that you should try to see the dream as representing different parts of your own life. You see yourself in the dream and not only this, you see parts of yourself and your life which are normally unconscious.

The dream tells you things about yourself and your future which you would otherwise not know.

The Dream Dictionary

A dream dictionary is a useful tool for learning about the archetypal, the common interpretations of dream symbols. Make sure you obtain one that is as comprehensive as possible, and I can even recommend obtaining more than one. If you do this, there is more chance of finding an interpretation of the symbol that you are looking up. Also, if there is an overlap and the dictionaries each carry the same entry, you are sure to find extra information about the symbol that interests you.

Because the dream dictionary only deals with the common interpretations and cannot give you any personal ones, it has limited value. This problem can be solved by making your own dictionary.

Make a list of all the images that appear in your dreams, keeping them in alphabetical order. Against each entry write a short interpretation, a personal one, what the symbol means to you.

This exercise bears fruit as time goes by. First, you will be able to look back to see if your feelings about what a dream symbol meant to you have changed, and as you collect symbols you will see which ones are easy to interpret, which seem to keep their meaning hidden from you, which occur regularly and which occur perhaps only once.

Your Dream Diary

A dream diary could be an extension of the idea of making your own dream dictionary. Use the diary in the same way that you would a normal diary, but in addition to this make the dictionary a part of it, so that when you enter a symbol in the dictionary, you can add the date that it occurred and also a reference linking it with a description of the dream in which it occurred.

One of the great benefits of keeping a dream diary is that the memory of dreams will quickly fade but a written record will not. Also, something occurring in a dream that does not seem immediately obvious may become so with the passage of time.

Finally, dreams often have a pattern which only becomes obvious when they have been recorded over a period of time, so keeping the diary will actually help in your understanding and interpretation.

Now that we have delved into the workings of the conscious mind and the psychic experience, then going further into the unconscious and the role played by our dreams, it is time to continue our journey into the future, armed with all that we have learnt so far.

Make a list of all the images that appear in your dreams.

Going further into the unconscious and the role played by our dreams. . .

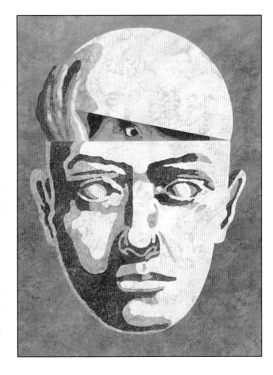

Dowsing with Pendulum Power

You can use dowsing to delve into your own future. This has been made possible by the use of different tools, especially the pendulum, which is most effective.

The image conjured up by the word dowsing is of someone walking through fields and woods pointing a forked branch in front of them waiting for it to jerk up or down at the crossing point of water or minerals beneath the earth.

Traditionally, the practice of dowsing is just this but the art has been extended in recent times into new domains, including the use of dowsing for foretelling the future. In this chapter we are going to investigate the whole field, how dowsing works, how it is done and how you can use it to delve into your own future. This has been made possible by the use of different tools for dowsing, especially the pendulum, which we will find is most effective.

What is Dowsing?

Dowsing is the reaction caused by some hidden object on a person, the dowser, who may employ certain tools to amplify the effect of the object. Dowsing has a particular characteristic. Although there is a chain of cause and effect in the dowsing process, the link between cause and effect is not at all obvious, if indeed there is any physical link at all.

An example of dowsing is where the dowser uses a forked stick, usually cut from a hazel tree, and walks with the stick, holding a branch in each hand. The dowser holds in his mind the object that he is looking for – perhaps water, perhaps minerals or something else buried under the ground and therefore invisible – until he feels the stick reacting, moving in his hands, perhaps jerking up or down. At that point the dowser knows that he is standing over the object that he is looking for.

Perhaps there is some undetectable force acting on the stick, perhaps it is the dowser unconsciously moving the stick in response to a reaction in his unconscious mind. The argument rages on between dowsers in different camps.

How Dowsing Works

In the example quoted above, the dowser tries to find something which is invisible to the physical senses. The stick is used to amplify the reaction caused by the object. The dowser is involved in this process because he holds in his mind an image or thought of what it is that he is trying to locate or 'divine'. These are the essential ingredients.

It is significant that dowsing is also called 'divining' which is exactly what we are doing when delving into the future. An oracle for predicting the future is also described as a divining tool and the process of looking into the future is called divination. Looking into the future assumes that there are invisible links between the future and the present, in just the same way that the dowser assumes that there is an invisible link between his mind and the stick on which the object can make its presence known.

From a book first published in Halle (Germany) in 1700. The dowser is shown twisting the nose of a symbolic image of the city.

So, what we are going to do is apply the technique of dowsing not for looking for things hidden under the ground, but for events hidden in the future.

Girl dowsing with a forked branch.

Trying It Out

First, here is an experiment for you to try. Ask someone to bury an object, perhaps in your garden. They can tell you what the object is but not where it is buried. Now take a forked stick, hazel preferably for its elastic qualities. Point the stick straight out in front of you and hold each end in such a way that if the stick wanted to it could move up or down.

Hold an image of the object in your mind and then walk around until you feel the stick reacting by moving in your hands. At this point you should be standing directly over the object you are looking for. Dowsers experience quite strong reactions so it is not a question of being sensitive but of allowing the stick to move when it wants to – let it have a mind of its own.

You will find that you can locate your object in this way. The main thing is to keep an open mind and try it out for yourself. There are no guarantees that it will work every time, but dowsing, perhaps more than any other divination system, convinces many sceptics that there are more things in heaven and earth... Remember that to the true scientist it is the results of the experiment that matter not the theory, and if the results do not fit the current theory then perhaps it needs revising.

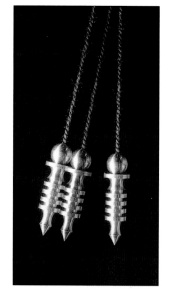

A pendulum consists of a weight or 'bob' at the end of a thread, usually about ten centimetres long, which is free to swing.

Hold an image of the object in your mind.

Using a Pendulum

The method used above is quite cumbersome. Waving a large forked stick around is not really appropriate for divining the future! There are other dowsing tools available and the most appropriate is the pendulum. This consists of a weight or 'bob' at the end of a thread, usually about ten centimetres long, which is free to swing.

The idea is that you hold a question in your mind and the pendulum will respond with an answer. The answer to your question will be related to the direction that the pendulum begins to circle, either in a clockwise or anticlockwise direction. The question must therefore be phrased in such a way that it needs a yes or no response. The pendulum won't go into details!

You can use anything as your pendulum, common bobs being made from wood or cut glass crystals. The advantage of a pendulum is that it is not cumbersome and can be used without you walking around.

The emphasis on this type of divining is in seeking the answer to a question, rather than looking for a hidden object, although you could say that the answer to your question is hidden in the unconscious, rather than being underground.

Exploring the Hidden Powers of Your Mind

Hold your pendulum and let it settle until it is quite still. Then ask it a question to which you know the answer. For example, if your name is John Smith, ask the pendulum if this is your name and wait for it to begin to swing in a circle. The point of this is that the direction in which it swings gives you your positive direction – you know now which way it will move to give a 'yes' answer. The other direction represents 'no'.

Now you are ready to divine using your pendulum. The applications are legion. Here is a good use to put it to. You could ask it questions about your diet. Is cabbage good for you? See which way it swings.

It is clear at this point that the yes/no response is limited, because you need to ask a precise question. It's no good asking which

food will be best for you as the pendulum can't say 'cabbage' or 'apples'. There is a way round this by asking your questions in groups and then narrowing down the possibilities. For example, you could ask first, is it fruit? No. Is it vegetables? Yes. Is it a common vegetable? Yes. Is it green? Yes. Etc., etc. This method keeps you on the right track until you narrow the answer right down to only one possibility.

Another trick which dowsers use is to have a 'witness'. This is an object which is related to the question. For example, to find which food is best suited to someone else, ask them first for a sample of their hair, or something which is personal to them. Hold this 'witness' while divining so that a link can be made with this person.

The French Universal Pendulum, patented in France in 1936 and available today. It is said to be capable of emitting electromagnetic and electric waves.

Brain Rhythms

Yet again we are seeing common ground with other divination systems: the need to clear the mind and focus it, being open to whatever comes; the need to formulate a clear question so that the response is clear; the ability to delve beneath the surface using the power of the mind, ignoring the limits of everyday reality.

Dowsers often discuss their responses indicated by wave emissions from the brain. Different forms of consciousness produce different electromagnetic emissions as can be clearly demonstrated by measurement using an electroencephalograph machine. The emissions are tiny but have definite characteristic rhythms or frequencies.

The frequencies of emissions have been categorized into beta waves (13-30 Hz), alpha waves (8-12 Hz), theta waves (4-7 Hz) and delta waves ($\frac{1}{2}$-4 Hz). Beta waves are associated with normal activity, the performance of physical and mental tasks. Alpha waves are associated with states of deep relaxation. Theta waves are associated with reverie, with meditation, with dreaming and the states experienced when entering or coming out of sleep. The slowest, delta waves, are associated with dreamless sleep.

Meditation and psychic experience are associated with the alpha state, and we can add to this now the experience of pendulum dowsing.

Translucent pendulum.

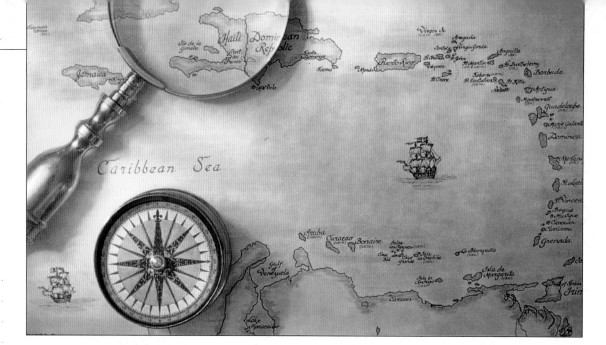

You can dowse at a distance, and it would appear that the effect is not diminished by long distances.

Questions and Answers

It would appear that pendulum dowsing is the answer to all our needs. As long as you can formulate a question that can be answered by yes or no, then there is nothing that you can't discover. However, this is not the end of the story. We are dealing here with divining and are bound by the same rules that apply to all our other systems of divination.

In just the same way that an answer given by a Tarot card or a dream cannot necessarily be taken literally, so too must we be careful about the answers provided by our pendulum. If this was a completely objective system which did not include in it the effect of the human mind, then dowsing would simply be a science whose effects were directly measurable, repeatable and provable. Indeed, some dowsers would claim this. Our approach is to take into account the involvement of the mind, of the unconscious as we have done throughout the study of our relationship with the future.

It is impossible to separate out the 'dowsing effect' so that it can be measured. Who knows what other influences are at work when we are dowsing? Can other people influence the result, for example? When you consult your Tarot cards, you will find that sometimes your reading is good, is accurate, at others it will be puzzling. Dowsing is like this, too. The dowsing oracle has its own agenda which can affect the results.

Dowsing at a Distance

I started off this chapter by describing the traditional image of what dowsing is all about. Dowsers have rewritten the rule books over the years, so that dowsing can be very different from this. An interesting example is of dowsing at a distance. Rather than using a forked stick, the dowser uses a pendulum, and rather than walking about the fields and woods, he, or she, uses a map.

The dowser simply runs a finger over the map, holding in mind an image or thought of what it is that he wishes to find, while holding the pendulum in the other hand. As the finger passes over a 'hot spot', the pendulum begins to swing, suggesting to the dowser that this is where the buried object lies.

The consequence of this is that you can dowse at a distance, and it would appear that the effect is not diminished by long distances. This would suggest that other divining systems, the oracles that we have been considering, are not affected by distance in any way. There are disadvantages in doing postal readings, for example, because it is difficult to get direct feedback to the material that crops up, but the accuracy of a reading for someone at the other end of the country should not be affected simply by physical separation.

Divining the Future

To use dowsing for delving into the future is the final step to take. It is simply a matter of putting your pendulum to use after formulating the appropriate questions. As long as you need no more than a 'yes' or a 'no', you are ready to start exploring.

You may find that the best use you can make of dowsing is in conjunction with other oracles, when you can use it to clarify anything which does not seem clear to you. For example, a Tarot card may suggest that something will happen in the future but seems not to be clear about the timing of the event.

Dowsing for further information would be a matter of narrowing down the possibilities in the way that I described above. Ask, 'Will it happen in the next year?' If the answer is yes, 'Will it happen in the first half of the next year?' If the answer is no, 'Will it happen in the third quarter of the next year?' If the answer is yes, 'Will it happen in the seventh month of the next year?' And so on, until you pinpoint the exact date.

There is a temptation with dowsing to try and catch it out by asking questions to which you know the answer. Apart from the initial setting up, when you determine which direction of the pendulum swing represents yes, and which no, you will find that the system wont work well if you do this. Proof positive that the system works can be obtained over and over again by means of asking questions about the genuinely unknown, when you will later discover for yourself the accuracy of your divined answers.

Different Applications

Before leaving this chapter, and because you may well wish to explore the possibilities of dowsing further, there are several other interesting and related applications.

The main one of these is in the field of health. I indicated in an earlier chapter on psychic explorations that health was often an important issue when developing the psychic sense. Dowsing is a potent tool for exploring your needs and the needs of other people in this area. I have already mentioned the application to diet, but in addition to this it is possible to seek out allergies or bad reactions to particular foods by consulting your pendulum.

You may have heard of geopathic stress whereby ones constitution can be affected by geological environmental factors, underground rock formations, minerals, water flows, etc. Dowsing for these influences is one way of discovering such negative or positive influences – rather like dowsing for the presence of underground objects but in this case you are seeking out their effects on you.

Ley lines and power points in the earth, often associated with ancient religious sites, provide much fodder for dowsers. Remember, you can dowse for the past as well as the future, so that your dowsing could throw light on people and places that existed before the dawn of history.

There are several other interesting and related applications. The main one of these is in the field of health.

Magic of the Runes

Detail of runic inscription on the famous Jelling Stone (E. Jutland), said to have been raised by King Harald Bluetooth to his parents, Gorm and Thyra, circa 985.

One of the most ancient of oracles still in popular use today is that of casting the runes, a system which has come down to us from the esoteric tradition of Northern Europe, a tradition which goes back as far as Viking times.

Runic practice includes making and casting the runes for predictive purposes, and the making of amulets, talismans, and runic monograms. Like other oracles, such as the Chinese Book of Changes, which we will investigate in the next chapter, the runes can be much more than just a simple oracle, offering both a complete system of rune magic, and a philosophy about life and its purpose. Behind the runes lies the power of Nordic mythology and the tales of its gods and goddesses.

The Ancient Art of Casting the Runes

The runes consist of a set of ancient sigils or signs, each one traditionally marked on a small stone. Today, most rune users work with 24 runes. This is known as the Common Germanic Futhark or the Elder Futhark, evidence of which dates back to the fifth century. The Elder Futhark is the oldest and most widespread runic system. Although stone is the traditional material from which the runes are made, it is common to find sets made from ceramic material, or the runes are often carved into wood. To make a set is therefore quite simple, and to get started straight away, you could even mark the sigils on small individual pieces of card.

As a divination system, the runes are used in just the same way as might be the Tarot. The particular runes which crop up, or are 'cast' in a reading, being determined by the gods of fate and chance. Each rune has its own meaning and interpretation. The magical power of the runes lies not only in their individual meanings, but also in the possibility of combining them – remember that with our Tarot cards the relationships between the cards in a spread were significant. The word 'rune' refers to some aspect of the mysterious inner structure of existence.

Where the Runes Came From

A Norse legend records how Odin, the god of magic, obtained the power and meaning of the runes for human use through an initiation of shamanic proportions:

> *I know that I hung on the*
> *windswept tree,*
> *For nine days and nine nights,*
> *I was pierced with a spear, and*
> *given to Odin,*
> *Myself given to myself,*
> *On that tree, which no man knows,*
> *From which roots it arises.*
> *They helped me neither with bread,*
> *Nor with drinking horn.*
> *I took the runes.*
> *Screaming, I took them,*
> *Then I fell back from that place.*

Fortunately, in order for us to understand the runes we need not undergo the same torments as Odin. His ordeal was to hang from a tree, enduring pain, hunger and thirst for nine days and nights, a magically powerful period of time. His torment was concluded by a flash of insight as the secret knowledge of the runes fell to him.

How the Runes Work

First you will need to make a background onto which you can cast your runes. Take a cloth and draw on it three concentric circles as shown. Each ring represents a different area of life. In the example shown, the outer ring represents future events, the middle ring represents influences, and the centre ring represents the inner self.

There are other possibilities for the meaning of the rings. An alternative could be: outer ring, 'doing'; middle ring, 'thinking'; centre ring, 'being'. Sometimes runemasters suggest that the area outside the three rings is not important and can be ignored, but I prefer to think of it as the 'ice' area. A rune falling here indicates that what it represents is literally 'frozen', is put on ice, is tucked away in storage.

Having created your background onto which you can cast the runes, you now have the means of creating the equivalent of a Tarot spread. When you cast the runes onto the cloth they will fall into one of the three circles, or will end up outside all three. Your runes are then ready for an interpretation.

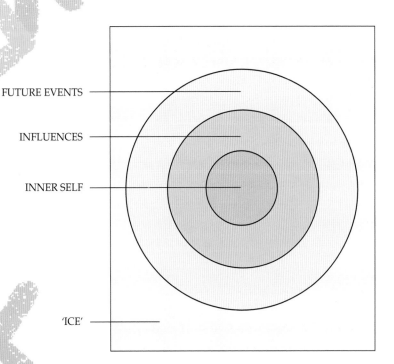

FUTURE EVENTS

INFLUENCES

INNER SELF

'ICE'

Rune Symbols & Meanings

Feoh:	The price to pay	
Ur:	Obstacles	
Thorn:	Petty annoyances	
Os:	Something important to be said	
Rad:	Long overdue change	
Ken:	Listen to your inner voice	
Gufu:	A gift or sacrifice	
Wynn:	Joy and separateness	
Hoel:	Someone else's battle	
Nyd:	Needs may not be met	
Isa:	Indicates no movement	
Ger:	A time of natural change	
Eoh:	The 'limitations' rune	

Poerdh:	The roots of a mystery
Eolh:	Inspiration; health and safety
Sighel:	Good luck; time for a change
Tir:	Time to get things moving
Beorc:	Formation of close relationships
Ehwis:	Assistance required from others
Manu:	Strengths and weaknesses
Lagu:	Trust your feelings
Ing:	Rune of withdrawal; fertility and marriage
Odel:	Practical issues to sort out
Doerg:	On the right path

Runic Correspondences

Now that you have been introduced to the runes, it is worth taking a step back in time to explain a little more about the origins of runic lore. It is possible that the runes have a common ancestry with prehistoric rock carvings used by the Neolithic and Bronze Age peoples of Old and Northern Europe. It has been suggested that the sharp angular strokes of the runes are due to the fact that they were originally carved in stone. Such a method of recording an ancient script or alphabet would inhibit the use of rounded or curved sigils.

Dating from later times, runes have been found carved on wood, metal and bone. They are divided into three families, or 'aettirs', each family containing eight runes. The three families are each attributed to a particular god. Each rune is also assigned a numerical value between one and eight, and a colour. When interpreting the runes, it will give a greater understanding if you compare the meanings of all the runes with the same number.

It becomes evident now that the runes, like astrology and the Tarot, and indeed other divination systems, are based on a system of correspondences, each rune governing, or ruling its own particular areas, objects, colours, numbers, plants, gods, etc.

Rune stones.

Casting and Interpreting the Runes

Let's now use your rune oracle. I will assume that you have obtained a set of runes, but if you haven't it is quite easy to make a set (see page 67). Spread your cloth with the three circles representing future events, influences and the inner self.

There are several ways of casting the runes, and the number of runes that you cast at a throw can vary too. It is usual to cast either three, six, or nine runes, but you can experiment to find out what works best for you. Let's say that you choose to cast three runes. Put your runes in a bag and shake them around to mix them up and while you do this formulate a clear question to ask the runic oracle. Draw out a rune without looking at it. Take another rune, and then a third.

Next, hold them over the centre of your circle. Hold your question in your mind as you drop the runes onto the circle. Let them bounce and roll to settle where they will.

Now you can interpret the runes according to their meanings, and according to where they fall on the circles, looking also for relationships between them. Are there, for example, any common themes that come out of your interpretation? Remember to use your intuition as well. Let your psychic imagination play its part.

Some of the runes may have fallen face down, with their blank side upward. This suggests that what the rune represents is currently hidden or perhaps suppressed.

Three rune stones, from left to right: **Feoh** *(the price to pay),* **Tir** *(time to get things moving) and* **Ing** *(withdrawal, fertility and marriage).*

Runesticks being used by magicians. Plate from Olaus Magnus, *1658 translation of 'A Compendious History of Goths, Swedes and Vandals'.*

Odin himself advised his followers what they could expect to learn if they followed him on the shamanic path:

> *Ye shall find runes and*
> *signs to read,*
> *signs most might, signs so strong,*
> *which the soothsayer coloured,*
> *the High Gods made,*
> *and the old Ones carved.*

Amulets and Talismans

The ancient runic tradition as a complete system of magic was used for purposes other than as an oracle. One such use was to provide amulets and talismans. A Runemaster would choose special runes to bring their wearer protection from evil, or perhaps to bring wealth and good fortune. The runes could be used to promote fertility or success in battle.

Many ancient objects still exist to show us the techniques of historic rune magic. Wood was used extensively for carving the runes, which is why relatively few wooden examples remain today. There are, however, survivors, including the Ribe Healing Stick, a pine-wood stave, 30 cm (12 inches) in length, carrying a runic spell to exorcise the disease called 'The Trembler', which is thought to be the old name for malaria.

Runic words of power are composed of a number of runes. In certain combinations, these are the Names of Power, which come mainly from Old Norse and Anglo-Saxon early runic languages. Their use is a means of accessing the power that the names represent. Each Name of Power has a numerological value, an interesting addition to our knowledge about the power of names and numbers.

The Rune Masters

Anyone today who masters the use of the runes and their esoteric language becomes a potential 'Runemaster'. A Runemaster is a descendant of the prehistoric shamans who gained their power by means of initiation into the reality of other worlds, of other states of consciousness. The Runemasters, like the Northern European shamans, were able to communicate with the spirit world through their psychic powers.

In order to communicate with these other dimensions initiates could achieve the state of ecstatic trance by ritual dancing, chanting and drumming. These techniques can be traced to have a link with the runic system as ritual drums used by Finnish and Siberian shamans often had mystical symbols painted on them which are almost identical to the runic alphabet.

Making Your Own Runes

Collect 24 flat pebbles, about 2 cm (3/4 inch) in diameter. On one side of each, mark a rune sigil but leave the other side blank. Use a felt or marker pen. Collecting your stones should be a meditative experience. Personally, my ideal is to do this on the sea-shore. Have you ever looked by the sea for pebbles with interesting shapes, colours and patterns? Now is your chance to put them to good use.

I mentioned that wood is also a popular material and all you need is a tree branch about 2 cm (3/4 inch) in diameter which can be sawn up into 24 'pebbles'. The advantage of making wooden runes is that you can customize them easily, smoothing them, staining them, perhaps burning the runes into the wood with a soldering iron, and finally varnishing the surfaces to keep them clean.

I suggested shaking up your runes in a bag before casting them so you could make or purchase a special draw-string bag in which to keep them, together with the cloth on which the runic circles are marked.

Whichever way you make your runes, remember that in each of them there is a little bit of yourself, so treat them with respect, work with them regularly and get to know them intimately as your friends and allies.

The advantage of wooden runes is that you can customize them easily.

Developing Runic Skills

As with all the oracles that we have explored so far, the power of your runes to reveal the future will grow as you work with them. You will find that the meanings of the runes have great depth and are also open to interpretation, so feel free to develop your own, as you experiment with different methods for casting and reading them.

Although the basic meanings of the sigils have to be learnt to get you started, once you have done this you will find it relatively easy to develop your knowledge about each one. This will come about first by reading more about the runes but mainly through using them – the runes will eventually begin to communicate to you their meaning. This is what you are aiming at. When this begins to happen, when the runes themselves tell you what they mean, you will know that you are being initiated into a great secret.

Rune stones around a scrying glass.

The Inscrutable I Ching
Chinese Divination

The Pa Qua, or eight trigrams, on the back of a Dragon Chair.

*A*lthough the *I Ching* was introduced into the west in relatively recent years, it has a history which is far older than that of any of the oracles we have considered so far, with the possible exception of astrology. The *I Ching* is based on the idea that the universe follows fixed laws and patterns, thus making the future entirely predictable and knowable.

However, it also has another special characteristic which will help us in our search for the ultimate oracle. The *I Ching* does not describe specific future events but suggests to its user the changes that are taking place at the time it is consulted, and where these changes are leading in the future. Hence, the meaning of *I Ching* is 'The Book of Changes'.

The Book of Changes

The *I Ching* is appropriately named the Book of Changes for it records the changes that occur continuously in life. Nothing is static, everything is in a state of flux, all life is movement. More than this, the patterns of change are cyclic. Nature is a never-ending process of cyclic change, and so too is human nature. Thus, the *I Ching* describes the process of change. If you know where you are in life, then the *I Ching* records where you are going – and hence gives the appearance of predicting the future.

The philosophy behind the *I Ching* is that, knowing the changes that are taking place in your life, it is far more sensible to move with these natural forces than to move against them. Only by accepting the inevitability of, and conforming to, cyclic change can harmony, peace of mind and a satisfactory outcome be achieved.

Happiness follows sadness; sadness follows happiness; poverty follows riches; riches follow poverty; failure follows success; success follows failure. All the opposites are in a continuous interplay, a dance of perpetual movement. The *I Ching* will tell you where you are in the dance, suggesting to you the steps you can take to flow easily into the future. . .

The Book of Wisdom

The *I Ching* is more than just an oracle, it is a philosophy of life. To the Chinese it attained the status in their culture of a bible. The Chinese long believed in the mystical properties of nature. They observed cyclic change in the passing of the seasons and applied this to human behaviour. They believed also in the oneness of the universe and that everything was intimately interconnected, an idea that we have already come across when exploring other oracles.

This belief spawned a complete philosophy of life and inspired a moral code too. It was a duty to discover the changes so that the right course of action could be taken. Doing the right thing had an effect on the whole of the universe and added to the sum total of 'goodness' in the world. Certainly there is much more in the *I Ching* than just a means of predicting the future.

The *I Ching* encourages meditation by providing a greater awareness of the world and by teaching both self-knowledge and the art of forming relationships. So, the *I Ching* does not concern itself with trivialities. Instead, it directs the questioner's attention to alternatives, its answers showing the consequences of one's actions.

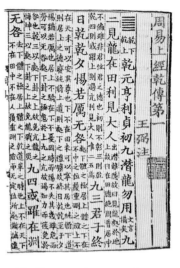

The first page from a tenth century woodblock edition of the Chinese classic I Ching.

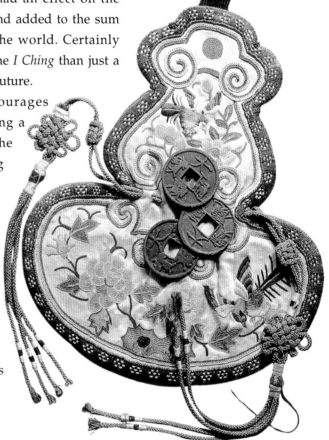

Above: Coins used in the art of divination with I Ching.

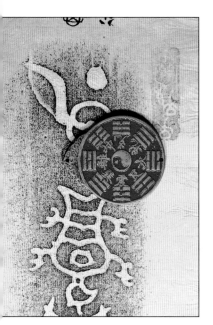

The Eight Trigrams

In 3322 BC, the Emperor Fu-hsi sought to differentiate between the two opposing forces of nature, Yin and Yang. He chose a broken line to represent Yin (– –), and an unbroken line to represent Yang (——). From these he created different combinations of three lines, each line being either Yin or Yang, resulting in eight 'Trigrams', seen below left.

Building the 64 Hexagrams

By placing two trigrams one above the other, it is possible to create 64 new combinations called the Hexagrams. The Hexagrams each have their own meaning, determined by the combination of Trigrams used in their structure. To give the meanings of all of the Hexagrams would be impractical in a book of this nature, nevertheless it is valuable to know how to consult the *I Ching*, particularly if you obtain an interpretation handbook for yourself.

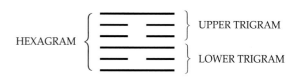

King Wen interpreted the meanings of the Hexagrams and composed 64 short essays to accompany them. These are what constitute the prophecies; they are called the 'Judgements'. The Hexagrams, together with the Judgements form the *I Ching*.

Trigram	Name	Attributes & symbols
☰	Chi'en	Creative, male, active: heaven
☷	K'un	Receptive, female, passive: earth
☳	Chen	Movement, perilousness: thunder
☵	K'an	Pit, danger: water
☶	Ken	Arresting progress: mountain
☴	Sun	Gentle penetration: wood, wind
☲	Li	Brightness, beauty: fire
☱	Tui	Pleased satisfaction: marsh, lake

Yin and Yang

The essence of the *I Ching* is the interplay of opposites which are called Yin and Yang. There is a famous symbol which describes this interplay.

Originally, Yin symbolized shade, Yang, light, and the concept of opposites was thus indicated. Yin was used to describe the female or passive elements, Yang, the male or active. In Western terms, Yin is negative, Yang, positive. Even in the human being, there is, at a fundamental level of the structure of the brain, a representation of Yin and Yang. The brain is divided into two hemispheres, and, generalizing, the left hemisphere determines the operation of our rational thinking, whereas the right hemisphere is associated with the imagination. Rationality is masculine and therefore Yang; imagination is feminine and Yin.

It does not matter on which level you approach the *I Ching* for it simply considers the relationships between the opposites and the way that one flows or changes into the other.

The relationship of Yin and Yang determines both our happiness and our health – an excess or deficit of either can lead to deterioration, while maintaining a correct balance brings good fortune.

The famous symbol which describes the interplay of opposites.

Consulting the I Ching

First, as in all our previous examples, you should frame an appropriate, clear question. The next part of the process is to find out which of the 64 Hexagrams is the one that illuminates the answer to your question. Traditionally, there are two ways of doing this, either by manipulating a quantity of yarrow stalks, or by tossing three coins of the same denomination. We will use the latter. Heads usually represent Yang, and tails Yin.

There are four types of lines that can be formed by a throw of three coins, as shown. The required Hexagram is constructed by the process of throwing the three coins six times. Each time you throw the coins, their value is added up (heads score 3, tails 2) and the corresponding line is drawn on a piece of paper. The first line is usually at the base of the Hexagram, which is constructed from the bottom to the top.

Referring again to the four possible lines, you will see that two of them are described as moving lines. This means that, if they crop up with reference to your question, the moving line is in the process of changing into its opposite – for example, you may score a 6 which is a broken but changing line. It is a Yin line about to change into a Yang line.

When you have thrown your coins six times, you will have constructed the hexagram which answers your question. However, if while doing this, one or more changing lines have occurred, then the interpretation is that your Hexagram is in a state of flux, is changing into a new Hexagram. The idea is that by changing the lines as indicated (Yin to Yang, and vice versa), you will create a new Hexagram. The interpretation of the new Hexagram tells you what the changes are leading to in the future.

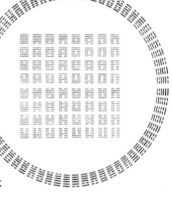

The 64 hexagrams arranged in both circular and quadrate form.

Coins show	Score	Represented by
3 Tails	6 (Moving Line)	——✕——
2 Tails, 1 Head	7 (Young Yang)	————
1 Tail, 2 Heads	8 (Young Yin)	—— ——
3 Heads	9 (Moving Line)	——◯——

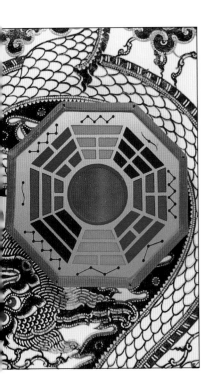

The eight trigrams of the I Ching *system, with corresponding 'constellation images', around a central mirror, intended to deflect the path of evil spirits. Such devices are usually hung on walls above windows or doors.*

Practising the consultation of the sacred Taoist text of the I Ching, *with the aid of yarrow stalks.*

The Judgement

You will find in the *I Ching* that the first part of the interpretation of each Hexagram is called 'The Judgement' and this is the interpretation proper. Everything else is by way of commentary on the Judgement.

When choosing a version of the *I Ching* for your own use, remember that the original contains much ancient symbolism and imagery which is not appropriate for today. It is therefore appropriate to purchase a version with an accurate re-interpretation of the original. Many of these exist and often have the fault of losing the depth of the original *I Ching*, so take some time in choosing or you may be disappointed later.

The Judgement will describe the situation that surrounds your question and will give you the material you need on which to meditate further. The Judgement is the key to your answer, not the answer itself and should be contemplated, thought about, explored, so that its meaning becomes clearer.

Together with the Judgement you will probably find a commentary which will help you in this process of understanding its meaning.

The Image

The next part of the text associated with each Hexagram is described as 'The Image', or 'The Symbolism'. In this, the Judgement is given again but in the form of a picture or a symbol. This takes us right back again to one of our original discoveries, namely that an oracle talks to us in symbols, which have their own special language and method of communicating their meaning.

The symbols or 'Image' given by the *I Ching* provide you with exactly the sort of thing which your unconscious mind loves to play with. So, my suggestion is that when consulting the *I Ching*, you take the image that occurs with your Hexagram and, in a meditative state, close your eyes and picture it. Try and see a simple scene which depicts the Hexagram's symbol. Let it change and develop in front of your mind's eye.

Then you can interpret it according to the approach that we developed, to discover the meaning of dreams and the type of images that crop up in meditation. The *I Ching* is exactly in tune with our method for predicting the future, which underlies all of the oracles that we have examined.

The Lines

The Judgements form the heart of the *I Ching* but the most interesting insights are given by 'The Lines'. These are individual interpretations of the moving lines. The interpretation of a moving line not only depends on whether it is Yin changing to Yang and *vice versa*, but also on which position in the Hexagram it appears. Any of the six lines of which a Hexagram is composed could be a moving line.

The Judgement gives an overall picture; the Image provides appropriate symbolism and the interpretation of the moving lines describes the dynamics of the situation, the way the tide is flowing.

Now for the most interesting part of all. Before you finish your interpretation, take each of the moving lines and turn it into its opposite. Yin becomes Yang and Yang becomes Yin. This means that you can now redraw your Hexagram with the new lines in position and in effect you will have created a completely new one.

This means that the situation surrounding the question which you posed to the *I Ching* is changing and will change into a new set of circumstances described by the new Hexagram. Your future is revealed.

Looking for the 'Changes' in Life

The *I Ching's* effectiveness as an oracle is backed up by a complete philosophy of life based on the idea of relatedness and change. This view of the world is as relevant now as when the *I Ching* was first formulated more than 5000 years ago.

The *I Ching* teaches how the 'Chuntzu', or 'Superior Man', should behave. The proper and good life is achieved by the Chuntzu when his life is in harmony with the flux of Yin and Yang, and when he moves with the continuous advance and regression of the vital forces of nature.

The *I Ching*, like the other oracles we have considered, has a personality of its own and should be approached with respect, in the manner of a student seeking instruction from a respected tutor. The answers obtained from the *I Ching* may at first appear to be obtuse but further reflection on them will almost always prove worth while. You will then be in a clear position to chose between one course of action and another, knowing exactly what their outcome will be.

A complete philosophy of life based on the idea of relatedness and change. This view of the world is as relevant now as when the I Ching was first formulated more than 5000 years ago.

The Futurescope
Make Your Own Prediction Machine

The mind interacts with an oracle to create symbols and images of the future.

We have surveyed several different oracles, looking at how they work, how they are used to best effect. We have discovered underlying similarities and correspondences between these different methods of foretelling the future.

We have looked at the role played by the mind and the unconscious and the way that the mind interacts with an oracle to create symbols and images of the future. We have looked at cultures past and the wisdom that has come to us from these earlier times. We have considered the nature of time and the relationship of past, present and future. Now we can put all of this together to create the ultimate oracle – the Futurescope.

Putting It All Together

From my researches I have developed a simple and effective oracle which is easy to make and easy to use. The Futurescope embodies all the principles that we have uncovered governing the operation of other oracles such as the Tarot, numerology, astrology, the Chinese *I Ching* and so on. One of the difficulties with these popular oracles is that there is quite a lot to learn before you can use them to their full potential. Keeping this in mind, I devised an oracle which you can use effectively straight away.

The Futurescope is therefore easy to test. Not only is it instantly accessible, but it has been devised so that the insights it gives can be greatly enriched by any knowledge gained from other oracles. I will explain this further when I describe how to use and interpret the Futurescope.

It appears to be quite a simple device, and indeed it is from the point of view of making one and using it. The beauty of it lies in its potentials – it can be used straight away on this basic level quite effectively, but if you wish to develop it, the Futurescope suggests all sorts of possibilities for extending its use, because behind it lies the power of all the other oracles that we have considered.

Creating The Futurescope

The Futurescope consists of a circle divided into 12 segments, each segment being labelled and numbered as follows:

1	IDENTITY	+ve
2	POSSESSIONS	-ve
3	COMMUNICATION	+ve
4	HOME	-ve
5	CREATIVITY	+ve
6	WORK AND HEALTH	-ve
7	RELATIONSHIPS	+ve
8	TRANSFORMATION AND RENEWAL	-ve
9	EDUCATION AND TRAVEL	+ve
10	CAREER AND AMBITIONS	-ve
11	IDEALS AND SOCIETIES	+ve
12	THE HIDDEN	-ve

Each of these segments corresponds to one of the astrological houses and they occur in the same order as the houses are found in the horoscope. Each segment has also been labelled as positive or negative, odd numbers being masculine and outgoing, representing INCREASE, even numbers being feminine and receptive, representing DECREASE.

Each segment of the Futurescope has been labelled as positive or negative. Segment 10 is labelled Career and Ambitions.

Making Your Own Futurescope

The circle is divided into segments and labelled as described above. In addition, the disc is divided as shown in the illustration into concentric circles, five in all. The centre is labelled the PAST. The next circle is labelled the PRESENT, and the next is the FUTURE.

The outer two circles are labelled with each segment's corresponding number and a +ve or -ve sign, with the outermost circle carrying the names of the twelve houses. All that remains is to add a pointer which is free to move on its axis, a pivot positioned right in the centre of the circle.

My prototype was made from sturdy card and the concentric circles were differentiated with different colours, partly to make it look attractive but also to distinguish them easily. The pointer itself is also cut from a stiff card and mounted on the point of a drawing pin pushed through the centre of the circle from the back. To keep the pointer from coming off you can complete the job by pushing a small protector onto the point of the pin.

The diameter of the futurescope should be a minimum of about 15cm (6 inches), with a corresponding pointer of approximately 9cm (3 1/2 inches) in length. Ensure that the pointer will spin freely when you give it a push and you now have your own working model of a Futurescope.

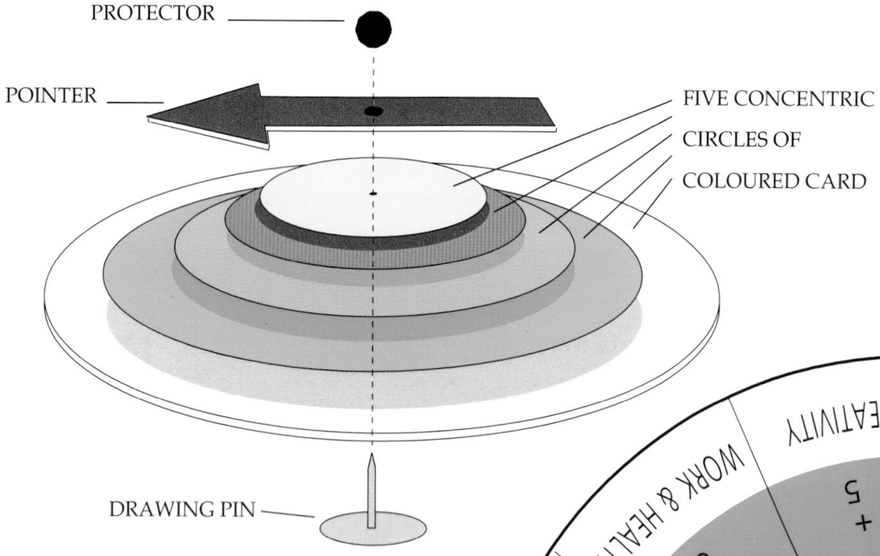

PROTECTOR

POINTER

FIVE CONCENTRIC CIRCLES OF COLOURED CARD

DRAWING PIN

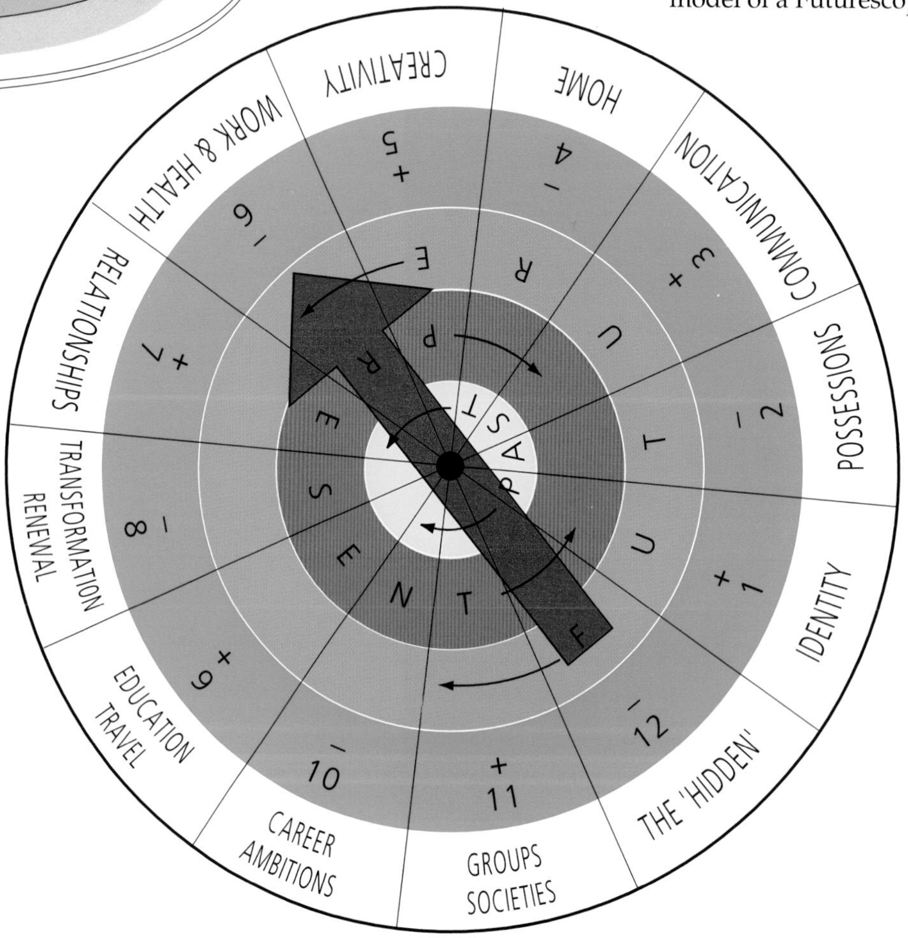

A simple and effective oracle, The Futurescope is easy to make and easy to use. It embodies all the principles that we have uncovered governing the operation of other oracles such as the Tarot, astrology, numerology and the Chinese I Ching.

How The Futurescope Works

The oracle is consulted three times when a question is put to it. The first time to determine influences that are coming from the past; the second time to determine the present situation; the final time to determine the future. Hold a question in your mind and spin the pointer. Where it comes to rest is determined by the winds of fate. There are three spins associated with determining the past, three spins for the present and three for the future. From these you will build up a picture in response to your question.

Here is how it works. To determine past influences:

1st spin: note down which house the pointer indicates
2nd spin: note down which number the pointer indicates
3rd spin: note down if the pointer indicates +ve or -ve

Repeat the process to determine present influences:

1st spin: note down which house the pointer indicates
2nd spin: note down which number the pointer indicates
3rd spin: note down if the pointer indicates +ve or -ve

Finally, repeat the process to determine the future outcome:

1st spin: note down which house the pointer indicates
2nd spin: note down which number the pointer indicates
3rd spin: note down if the pointer indicates +ve or -ve

Interpreting the Futurescope

Each time you consult the Futurescope you will have made three spins. For example, when consulting the past, from the first spin you note down the house, and this tells you where past influences are coming from.

From the second spin you note down the number. Simply look up the numerological interpretation of this number on page 38 and it will describe the quality of past influences. If the number that crops up is either 10, 11 or 12, these should be reduced numerologically, so that they become 1, 2 and 3 respectively.

Finally, the third spin indicates whether influences from the past are positive or negative. You can interpret this as 'bad' or 'good' if you like, but in the spirit of the I Ching, these can also be interpreted as +ve equals outgoing and creative (masculine), whereas -ve suggests receptive and introspective (feminine).

The next three spins give you information about the present, where influences are coming from, what their quality is and whether they are positive or negative. The final three spins describe future influences, their qualities and whether the outcome will be positive or negative.

The final three spins describe future influences.

Trying It Out

Let's say your question is, 'Will my current job be successful?' Here is an example of what might happen when you consult the Futurescope.

The first three spins relate to past influences. Let's say the first spin indicates 'Possessions', the second indicates the number '6', and the third '+ve'. You can interpret this as indicating that in the past you have known exactly what you have been doing (the number 6 represents insight and wisdom) in terms of gaining material possessions and that the influence has been a creative one of increase.

The next three spins relate to your current situation. Let's say the first spin indicates 'Work and Health', the second indicates the number '11' which reduces numerologically

You can interpret this as meaning that your current work and general well being are suffering from some tension and conflict of interests.

to the number '1+1=2', and the third '-ve'. You can interpret this as meaning that your current work and general well being are suffering from some tension and conflict of interests (the number 2 represents duality) and the influence is not a constructive one.

The final three spins relate to the future outcome. Let's say the first spin indicates 'Communication', the second indicates the number '3', and the third '-ve'. This means that you need to communicate any difficulties to other people in your work environment with the result of a resolution of any of your problems (the number 3 is the number of balance and resolution), but as the outcome is -ve you should not expect any increase in your fortunes in the immediate future.

Deeper Insights

You now have the means at your disposal for foretelling the future with a device that is immediately accessible. The basic interpretations that I gave to the example 'consultation' were brief but to the point. After trying out the Futurescope in this way, you can then start to explore further and expand on your interpretations.

Remember to open your intuitive faculties and accept the indications of the Futurescope in a spirit of openness and enquiry. The results may seem enigmatic at first but will reveal their penetrating insights with careful consideration and meditation.

You can expand on the results by investigating further, for example by learning more about the meanings of the astrological houses, and the significance of the number symbolism. Even the idea of +ve and -ve can be taken further by investigating the *I Ching's* attitude to the masculine/feminine polarities of Yin and Yang which I described in the previous chapter.

Links With Other Oracles

In addition to a new oracle which is simplicity itself to use, you also have the means at your disposal for exploring in as great a depth as you require, the meaning of the Futurescope's revelations.

I hope it has become clear how its development has grown out of an exploration of other methods for foretelling the future. The Futurescope's relationship with astrology is through its twelve divisions into different areas of influence, equivalent to the twelve astrological houses.

The method of considering past, present and future influences owes much to the Tarot spread which we considered, and the Futurescope's links with numerology are clear from its use of number symbolism. Even the *I Ching* plays its part with its insights into the interplay of positive and negative.

This is not all. The underlying 'rules' which support the workings of an oracle are applied to the Futurescope and are worth remembering here. Make your question clear and well thought out – an unclear question results in a confusing answer. While consulting the oracle, open up your intuition and psychic awareness so that you can respond to its indications with related insights of your own.

When your consultation is done, live with the ideas that have cropped up for a while; try to expand on their meaning and even meditate on them, allowing your unconscious to have its say.

Remember also that you should not ask the same question twice, unless the circumstances surrounding the question have changed. Accept what the oracle gives to you whether or not it is what you wanted, whether or not its meaning is clear to you.

Future Explorations

The applications of the Futurescope are limited only by your imagination. For example, it could be used to work out timings. Decide what unit of time each of the numbers represents, ask your question and spin the wheel. If you have decided on a unit of a week, then if the pointer indicates the number 3, say, then this represents three weeks.

The Futurescope can be used exactly like a divining tool. In answer to a yes/no type of question, the pointer will correspondingly indicate +ve or -ve, so that all we have said about dowsing with a pendulum now applies to this new universal device. We have created a system which combines in one astrology, Tarot, Numerology, the *I Ching*, and dowsing as well.

The dowsing element is extremely useful because, as long as you can formulate a question that requires a yes/no answer, you can use the Futurescope to clarify its own predictions. After a reading, after spinning to determine past, present and future, record the oracle's predictions and then use it again as a dowsing tool to clarify further what you have discovered.

Facing the Future

Having all the means at our disposal for predicting the future it simply remains for you to work on investigating your own, or that of your friends and associates.

There is another branch of prediction that we can turn to now that goes beyond the affairs of our personal lives. We can investigate the world of the great seers and prophets who dealt not with personal matters but with those affecting the future of countries and of the world itself.

Great Prophets, Great Prophecies

Perhaps predictions of future disasters are justified, perhaps not, only time will tell.

The end of a century is always marked by predictions of doom and disaster, even more so when we come to the conclusion of a millennium. Ours is an age of great change and uncertainty. The rapid pace of technological change, threats to the environment, the changing political scene in east and west alike, economic uncertainty, all these add to a feeling of unease about the future.

Perhaps predictions of future disasters are justified, perhaps not, only time will tell for most people. We, however, are in a position to consider the art of prophecy and will begin this final section with a look at those people of the past who have become famous for their prophetic visions of the future.

Great Prophets of the Past

Prophecy means to 'speak by divine inspiration', and a prophet is someone who speaks about revelations received from a divine source. There are some significant differences between prophecy and divination. Most notably, prophets do not choose to receive revelations about the future and often resist this role. They feel that they have been chosen as a vessel or transmitter for their prophecies, whereas divination is done as a matter of choice. Also, divination is usually conducted in response to a particular question, while prophecy happens spontaneously. Prophets are often unaware of the significance of their transmissions.

This does not mean that prophecy and divination are incompatible. Despite these differences there are also strong similarities. Both involve tapping into the unconscious mind in a state of relaxed awareness, both diviner and prophet opening themselves up to be a channel for whatever will or will not pass through them. Great prophets of the past have achieved infamy usually for the accuracy of their prophecies, but occasionally because of the opposite! Some have made prophecies which extend into the coming years and all seem to agree that we are in for a time of great change and upheaval.

Psychics, Seers and Mystics

A criticism of prophecies is that they are not specific and are open to interpretation. In some cases this is true to the extent that any interpretation can be made of the prophecy and it becomes impossible to determine whether or not it can make any claims to have revealed anything at all. There is an important point to be made here which emphasizes what we have discovered about the language of divination. Great prophecies are neither exactly specific, nor are they generalizations. They are given in the language of symbols.

This means that they will contain two aspects. The first is an underlying truth which makes them significant for everyone, the 'archetypal' aspect. The second is that they also carry personal truths, so that we can read into them our own interpretations. The mark of a great prophecy is that it is both universally significant and works on a personal level too. This is the secret of the power of prophecy.

Perhaps the best known example is that of the 'Book of Revelations' contained in the Christian Bible, which speaks in a language that is the stuff of dreams and nightmares. It seems clear then that its prophecies should not be interpreted literally but in the manner that we have developed to understand the art of divination – and now can apply to prophecy.

St John, the visionary, with God and the Elders in the clouds over a Mediaeval town.

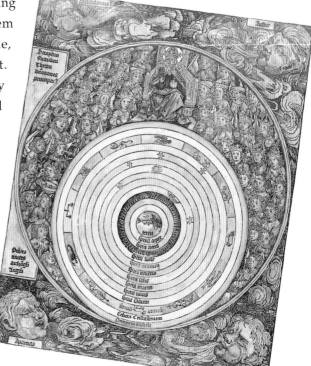

The Mediaeval cosmoconception, with God and his nine hierarchies looking down on to the world, in the centre of the Ptolemaic spheres, ringed by the zodiac. From a woodcut dated 1560.

quatrains were published in Nostradamus's *Centuries*, first appearing in 1555.

Interpreters suggest that Nostradamus has predicted a series of cataclysmic events which occur in the time approaching the millennium year of 2000. Commentators suggest that the year 2002 will see dreadful wars, while the world itself, according to Nostradamus, will come to an end in the year 3797. Astrologers confirm that planetary configurations over the coming years support Nostradamus's notions of natural and man-made disasters.

The Papal Prophecies of Malachy

Malachy O'Morgair, canonized as St Malachy, was born in the eleventh century. He created a series of short, enigmatic statements regarding the identity of the sequence of popes from his time until the end of the twentieth century.

The popes are given descriptions, such as the nineteenth century pope Leo XIII, who was described by Malachy as *'Lumen in Caelo'* (Light in Heaven), appropriately described for a man whose family crest was a comet. Pope Paul VI, whose coat of arms carried the fleurs-de-lys, was called *'Flors Florum'* (Flower of Flowers). John Paul I, whose reign lasted only 33 days, was *'De Medietate Lunae'* (of the Half Moon). He met his death in the middle of the lunar month, one month after taking office.

The present Pope John Paul II is *'De Labore Solis'* (Labour of the Sun or 'from the Lonely Labour'). Malachy lists two more popes to follow the present John Paul II. Using Malachy's timing, it is assumed that the end of the papacy will occur around the year 2000, a date which agrees with Nostradamus.

Michael Nostradamus (1503-1566) the prophet whose prophecies were first published in 1555 and are still well known today.

Nostradamus

Nostradamus is probably the best known prophet today, because his prophecies have proven to be of direct relevance for our lives in this century – and into the next. He stated that to avoid persecution he consciously jumbled the sequence and obscured the clarity of his prophecies.

This French prophet and astrologer received his prophecies in the form of images which he converted and wrote in the form of quatrains, four-line verses. These used a strange combination of ancient and modern languages, astrological and alchemical symbolism. The

Madame Blavatsky and Alice Bailey

Madame H.P. Blavatsky identified the spiritual masters Koot Hoomi, Djwhal Khul and the Master Morya as the transmitting sources of her books *Isis Unveiled* and *The Secret Doctrine*, which formed the foundation of the Theosophical Society in the western esoteric tradition.

The Englishwoman, Alice A. Bailey, had her first telepathic contact with 'The Tibetan', Djwhal Khul, in 1919. In the following 30 years she wrote nineteen books on a range of esoteric subjects such as healing, astrology, psychology and the science of the Seven Rays, all dictated by The Tibetan.

These women, and others, were channels for the transmission of the Secret Doctrine passed on for millennia within the Himalayas, fragments of which were periodically communicated to the outside world.

The Tibetan prophesied that a new age would begin to manifest in our time and what this means we will consider in the next and final chapter. His prophecies are accurate regarding the discovery and early use of atomic energy, medical advances and the general development of humanity.

Helena Petrovna Blavatsky (1831-1891), the founder of the Theosophical Society, and one of the greatest exponents of occultism of the 19th century.

Mother Shipton's Prophecies

Here's a tale with a lesson for us all, particularly relevant for the end of our century when great disasters have been predicted. Mother Shipton was a famous Yorkshire folk prophet who lived in a cave. The first recorded mention of her is in 1641. Her prophesies increased in number even after her death. She was credited with predicting the Great Fire of London amongst other political changes in England. One of her rhymes went like this:

The world to an end will come,
In sixteen hundred and eighty-one.

As the time approached, villagers throughout the north of England spent nights out in the fields confessing their numerous sins and crying for mercy, but the appointed time came and went. A revised prophecy appeared:

The prophecies of Mother Shipton, a reputed witch, were first published in a pamphlet in 1641.

The world will end we'll view,
In sixteen hundred and eighty-two.

Each year new prophecies appeared, were corrected and followed by another, until eventually, of course, they lost all credibility.

Edgar Cayce – the World's Greatest Psychic

The clairvoyant author, Edgar Cayce (1877 – 1945), who worked through trance to heal people, and who made many predictions about the future of the twentieth century.

Edgar Cayce was born on a small farm in the American state of Kentucky in 1877 and lived until 1945. He became renowned for providing expert material derived from psychic trance sessions on a wide variety of subjects, present and future. His belief was that there exists a form of universal mind which it is possible for the psychic to contact. This universal consciousness contains everything that comes to pass. It contains all knowledge. He called this the Akashic Record and the principle was that if you were in contact with the Akashic Record you would have access to information about anything at all, including the future.

Cayce's predictions were consistently gloomy. He predicted a series of cataclysmic events happening over a sixty-year span, leading up to the year 2000, but particularly from 1958 to 1998. He prophesied that the earth will be broken up in the western portion of North America; the greater part of Japan will go into the sea; the upper portion of Europe will be changed in the twinkling of an eye; land will appear off the east coast of America; open waters will appear in Greenland; upheavals in the Arctic and in the Antarctic will make volcanoes erupt in the torrid areas; land will appear between Tierra del Fuego and Antarctica; a shifting of the poles will encourage warmer climates.

The Popular Predictions of Old Moore

Old Moore holds a special place in the literature of prophecy. His almanac has been published continuously sinc 1697 and has been consistently popular perhaps never more so than today. *Old Moore's Almanac* provides an example of the state of the art of prophecy today. Its popularity does not reflect its reputation which is of an anachronism containing predictions which should not be taken seriously by any modern, rational person. Its 'downmarket' appeal is also suggested by the advertising which it carries, mainly catering for the superstitious and for those wanting a quick solution to problems of love or money.

Its predictions are often trite and although it is a big seller, it is derided by those who have no feeling for or belief in the art of prophecy. Nevertheless, Old Moore represents a tradition of astrological prophecy which stretches back into the Middle Ages and beyond, when such studies were taken seriously by peasant and academic alike.

Despite its poor image and a popularity based on sensationalism, Old Moore still carries a torch for the faith, and if you care to look into his almanac you will find that its world predictions are carefully and thoughtfully made, perhaps not by a mystic or seer but strictly according to traditional, seasoned, astrological principles.

Rudolf Steiner

Rudolf Steiner is perhaps best known for his alternative education system which has taken root in many countries. He was an early Theosophist who later created a whole philosophy called 'anthroposophy'. In this he formulated spiritual laws that govern our evolution and hence our future. Like Edgar Cayce, Steiner believed in the Akashic Record and our ability to tap into it through meditation and spiritual exercises.

His belief was that the ability to develop one's spiritual faculties and higher perception was possible through the study of his 'spiritual science', and that human development proceeded according to certain evolutionary laws. As a 'scientist of the spirit', it is possible to foresee future great world events and human destinies without interfering with the choices that are taken in the present.

Although there is much in Rudolf Steiner's work that is valuable for our understanding of human destiny and world events, anthroposophy is a difficult subject to comprehend and therefore perhaps fails to attract the following it deserves, needing a modern-day spiritual scientist to put Steiner's words into an accessible form.

Our Age of Uncertainty breeds fear and evermore people are all too ready to believe the prophecies of disaster.

The End of the World is Nigh (or Not)

Modern prophets of doom abound and will increase over the next few years. Our Age of Uncertainty breeds fear and evermore people are all too ready to believe the prophecies of disaster. It is true that our world for many is an unhappy place to live in, and that Armaggedon for someone somewhere is always happening right now. For many people it feels as if they are constantly living on the brink of disaster and if this is true in their personal lives, the tendency is to project this into the world which then appears itself to be on the brink.

There is another attitude which is taking hold, drawn by an equal force in the opposite direction. This opposite force speaks not of doom but of a New Age when all will become whole and healed, one world with people living in harmony whatever their beliefs. Perhaps we are at the pivotal point where things could go either way. Let us end on a positive note by investigating what the New Age is all about and whether or not we wish to create it and be a part of it.

The Age of Aquarius

Predictions for the Millennium

Each of the astrological ages lasts for about 2000 years or so.

Many sources, both religious movements and the great prophets of the past, indicate that we are coming to the end of an age and are preparing for the entry of a new one.

With this in mind and also remembering the predictions of great change in the years ahead, it seems clear that if we look at the changes that have occurred in our lives over the last century, then we ain't seen nothing yet!

What is meant by an age, where does the idea come from and what are to be the characteristics of the new one ahead? In this final chapter we will focus on predictions for the future, particularly those of a positive nature and what they will mean for us all.

What is the New Age?

Entering a New Age itself implies change, change of attitudes, change of beliefs, change of values and so on. Fundamental changes take place within individual people. The impulse for change comes from within, not externally from governments or religious organisations. Governments and religious groups usually impose their doctrine on people who follow it, as long as their guidance about how we should behave and what we should believe in, is relevant and makes sense.

At the end of an age, the opposite becomes true. It is a time when people loose faith in their political and religious masters. New beliefs take root, new religions – and governments – take a hold, growing in response to the changing needs of the individual.

The process is happening now as many people search for something in life which resonates with a ring of truth, hence the growing interest in 'alternatives', different ways of healing the sick, different beliefs in the nature of life and death, different ways of developing our society. But before the new can take hold, the old has to crumble away and this is the situation that we find ourselves in – the decline of civilization.

Entering the Age of Aquarius

From out of the decay of the old, arises the new, and this is taking place today too. A name for this new age has been given as the Age of Aquarius, which has its basis in astrological prophecies.

Each of the astrological ages lasts for about 2000 years or so. We are leaving the Age of Pisces and entering Aquarius.

When this change-over actually takes place has been a source of great debate amongst astrologers, and many different dates have been given. All this is irrelevant though, particular dates for when the change takes place are meaningless. The change is here with us now, today, and will continue for many years ahead.

The Piscean Age was the age of the great Christian religions and of those from the orient. The coming age is an age of humanity, not separated by beliefs or creeds. According to astrological predictions, from out of a period of great change, turmoil and violence will emerge a Golden Age, characterized by people living as individuals, with their own beliefs about the world, but living in harmony. Modern science is bringing us all closer together with its global communications network, encouraging this process.

A name for this new age has been given as the Age of Aquarius, which has its basis in astrological prophecies.

Native American Indian Prophecies

The Hopi prophets have foreseen the world wars, the invention of automobiles and aeroplanes and even the atom bomb.

The Hopi prophets have foreseen the world wars, the invention of automobiles and aeroplanes, and even the atom bomb, and that the sons of white men would live in communal societies.

They call these men and their kin, who would come to the elders to learn the healing arts, the 'Rainbow Warriors'. They are composed of every colour and race on the planet, as no pure blood remains in them. Part of their task is to show humanity that they are all the same, all members of the same tribe.

The Hopis wish that all such Rainbow Warriors will become spiritual warriors and help heal the Earth and restore the balance of nature. The great fear in our own societies is that such communal living will destroy our traditions and therefore our identity. This is an unfounded fear. Rather than destroying what we have created in the past, the Hopis suggest that we will create great respect for our heritage, whether this be respect for the natural world or for our cultural history.

Damage is done when we fear that this will be lost, and fight wars to protect it. Respect for the earth, respect for others and respect for ourselves as individuals is to be the keynote of the coming age. By joining together our resources and creating harmony between countries we will be able to deal with the world's problems as they exist today. As separate countries we will simply destroy one another.

Pyramid Prophecies

The second coming of Christ is predicted in many quarters.

It is more than a century now since Robert Menzies first advanced the theory that the proportions and measurements of the passage system of the Great Pyramid were a chronological representation of a prophecy, even though nothing was known about Egyptian messianic prophecies at the time. By equating the polar inch with the solar year, he reasoned that the Grand Gallery was the Christian Dispensation, beginning with the birth of Christ. He subsequently advanced the idea that the entrance doorway of the Ante-chamber symbolized the beginning of the final period of the great wars and tribulations prophesied in the Bible.

Messianic prophecies are quick to take hold of the popular imagination and indeed this is a characteristic prediction for the coming age. The second coming of Christ is predicted in many quarters. As in the time of the first coming, it is recognized that certain individuals are here to prepare the ground and act as focal points for the energies of the New Age. Some of these prophets may be true ones, but others are certainly false.

The Piscean Age was the age of Jesus Christ the man, the Aquarian Age is the age when the spiritual nature of the Christ can be realized in all of us. Perhaps this is what is meant by the second coming.

Predictions for the Next Century

The decline in influence of spiritual teachers in the last century has been accompanied by a movement towards people learning to trust their own inner resources. Science and technology are laying bare the secrets of the universe and even though science has investigated the workings of consciousness, the unconscious and the human mind, it has a long way to go yet.

Our understanding of the power of the mind is still in its infancy, but as more and more people realize that this power lies within us all, the more we will truly move into the next century.

The idea that we can all participate in the spiritual nature of Christ is part of this idea. It is a great threat to the established church orders that maintain their hold over the individual by acting as a spiritual intermediary. No longer will the priesthood hold its power as it will become simply unnecessary. Hence, one great prediction for the next century is that the power of the established churches will crumble.

That we can all participate in the spiritual nature of Christ is part of this idea.

Planetary Alignments

So how do the astrologers view our approach to the New Age? There are several significant indications in the relationships of the planets and constellations. One of the most controversial is an alignment of planets in a configuration known as a Grand Cross.

All of the planets will be clustered in and around the fixed signs of the zodiac which correspond to the four beasts of the Apocalypse – Taurus the bull, Leo the lion, Scorpio the eagle, and Aquarius the man. A date given as having particular significance, while this Grand Cross is occurring, is August 11, 1999, when an eclipse of the sun will take place in the fixed Fire sign of Leo.

The interpretation of this configuration is of extreme unrest and disorder, suggesting natural catastrophes such as earthquakes, tidal waves and eruptions.

The Uranus-Neptune conjunction of recent years and the entry of Pluto into the sign of Sagittarius, has been interpreted as a starting point for the great changes necessary to introduce the coming age. These particular planets and their configurations are symbols for feelings of unease within individuals who discover great difficulties to overcome in their lives. These difficulties are demanding that they change their way of looking at the world, reassessing their whole approach to their purpose in life.

All of the planets will be clustered in and around the fixed signs of the zodiac.

Earthquakes and Catastrophes

Yet again the image of earthquake and catastrophe occurs, this time in the astrological predictions. The 1970s saw the introduction of a period of unusually high numbers of incidents of major earthquakes and volcanic eruptions and this has in turn been related to an increase in sunspot activity, areas of turbulence in the sun's 'atmosphere'.

NASA studies support the fact that such solar activity increases significantly when Jupiter and Saturn – the two largest planets – are aligned in conjunction on one side of the sun. When these two planets take part in the Grand Cross of 1999 the result could be a major increase in sunspot activity followed by a corresponding increase in earthquakes and eruptions, some say even a disastrous tilting of the earth's axis.

. . . a major increase in sunspot activity followed by a corresponding increase in earthquakes and eruptions. . .

The conjunction of these two planets is a symbol of the 'Star of Bethlehem' showing the way to where the new incarnation lies. Perhaps this time they will shake things up so much that the only place we can look is within ourselves. In Jeffrey Goodman's *The Earthquake Generation*, it is predicted that the Gulf Stream will undergo a complex shift and that London will become a coastal town!

Psychic Predictions

Approaching the year 2000, Edgar Cayce and other psychics seem to agree on many of the changes that will take place. Some of these are as follows:

- There will be a shift of the Polar Axis.
- A new climate will be established.
- Ancient cities will be found in the wake of falling seas.
- There will be major disturbances on both coasts of the US.
- Major sections of the US will fall into the sea – a final coast-line will be established in Nebraska.
- There will be major earthquakes in Turkey.
- The Gulf Stream will undergo a complex shift.
- Some parts of the British Isles will submerge, while others will rise.
- Land will rise in the North Sea, as Norway, Sweden, Denmark and Finland will have repeated coastal inundations.
- Most of Hawaii and Japan will break away.

The New Jerusalem

After applying a numerological analysis of the Book of Revelations and also studying the number symbolism portrayed in such sacred monuments as are found at Glastonbury and Stonehenge, John Michell has proposed the idea of a coming New Jerusalem. He proposes that the Temple of Jerusalem, created from the geometry and cycles of terrestrial and lunar spheres, is a metaphor for the Earth itself, and that the restoration of the Temple is a rebirth of the Earth spirit and represents the return of the age of prophecy and the return of divine revelation.

Michell sees that underlying our current situation is a great struggle going on between two opposing forces, suggesting the same idea that occurs in the philosophy of Rudolf Steiner. Steiner interprets these opposing forces as representing on the one hand light, the spirit world and the urge to freedom, which he calls 'Luciferic', and on the other hand the forces of the dark, the earth and the urge to bind and limit, which he calls 'Ahrimanic'.

The New Age is characterized by the balancing of these opposing forces, for if either is dominant then the result is destructive. There are reflections here of the Chinese concept of Yin and Yang, described in an earlier chapter.

John Michell studied the number symbolism portrayed in such sacred monuments as are found at Glastonbury and Stonehenge, England.

Some Predictions of My Own. . .

The prophets are indicating catastrophic change, natural disasters, the demise of governments, the church, the papacy. We have a natural instinct that battles with itself, one side resisting change, the other forcing it on. And there is yet another factor which we have discovered in our exploration of what the future is all about and what it will hold for us.

I believe that the feeling for great changes comes not from the fact that these will necessarily take place in our outer world but will occur inside ourselves. The indications are that we are looking in the wrong place for where the changes will occur. It is a psychological fact that when something is stirring in us on an unconscious level, it tends to be projected into the outside world where it takes on a reality that seems to have no connection with us. This is an illusion.

I am sure that great outer changes will take place, for inner and outer worlds of experience are not separate, are related to one another, but the emphasis so far has been put too much on outer events and not enough on what is going on inside our own psyches. So, what is the nature of this inner revolution of consciousness which is bubbling away?

The Second Coming

Taking into account the prophecies regarding a second coming, and keeping in mind the characteristics embodied by the Age of Aquarius, the premonitions indicate an inner experience of the rebirth of the Christ spirit. Aquarius is the sign of man and suggests that new dimensions of awareness will be opened up to everyone and not just a chosen few.

In the Age of Pisces, the awareness of other dimensions of reality, of communicating with spirits (shamanism), has been held by relatively few people, the priests, gurus and teachers of the age. Aquarius represents a complete change where inner tuition will be the order of the day and all those religious institutions which have an intermediate priesthood will disappear.

The Second Coming will not be taken on by any single person but will be an experience in which we all can share. It represents a renewal of spiritual values and awareness but not in terms of the dogma of the old-age religions. Aquarius is an age of prophecy when all the faculties and abilities that we have explored in this book become facts of life and not supernatural superstition.

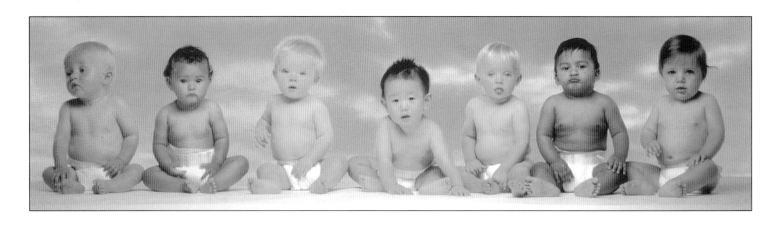

All this contributes to the growing sense that we are not separate from one another, that on the surface we look different, are individuals, but deeper down we all share common ground.

The Great Healing

From out of the destructive upheavals and dramatic changes that occur over the ensuing years, will come a new sense of healing and wholeness. There are signs of this already with the development of new forms of holistic healing which create an understanding of the mind/body relationship.

The healing will take place on all levels, from that of individual health, to that of the planet as a whole. We have a symbol for the oneness of mankind with the creation of information superhighways and the image of the earth as a single sphere taken from outer space.

All this contributes to the growing sense that we are not separate from one another, that on the surface we look different, are individuals, but deeper down we all share common ground. This process is enhanced by looking further than the surface. Surface appearances keep us apart, but inside we are all human beings, all live on and share the same earth, moon and sun.

The coming age will be one of brotherhood and sisterhood. There will be no loss of our individuality, simply an awareness of the depth of our being and hence our common ground.

Astrological Predictions – Aquarius

Aquarius is the age of ideals, of groups, countries, peoples, coming together and sharing common goals. The astrological indicators are for great change and I believe this to be an indication of inner change, to do with our consciousness and awareness, rather than an outer change to the environment.

Of course, in a holistic world the two go together, but my point is that the premonitions of destruction and disaster proclaimed by many prophets reflect fear of the unknown hidden inside ourselves. Certainly we have problems on our hands of a global scale, both political, social and environmental, but the solutions lie not in ideological beliefs but in an ability to see how we are all part of the solution and not the problem.

The symbol for Aquarius is the man pouring out waters from an urn, the waters of consciousness and awareness, meaning that in each of us lies a limitless well of potential. We can be who we want to be, create what we want to create, we have the power to do it, to pour out, to create our reality. It will no longer be governments and gurus who lead the people, but individuals everywhere will take their part in creating perhaps even a new civilization from out of the ashes of the old.

Aquarius is the age of ideals, of groups, countries, peoples, coming together and sharing common goals.

In Conclusion

Have fun with your Futurescope and your explorations of the times ahead. There is nothing unnatural about wishing to glimpse the future, particularly if it gives you an opportunity to change your life for the better.

Remember too that you are exploring new dimensions of reality which prophecies indicate will become more and more important and accepted as time goes on. If you are with me in exploring the nature of prediction and the relationship of past, present and future, then you are taking part in an exciting adventure. Outer space is not the final frontier, but inner space may be. You don't need a spacecraft to take this journey, just the will to find out more about yourself and an open mind as you take your own special journey into the future.

Bibliography & Recommended Reading

Almond, Jocelyn & Seddon, Keith, *Understanding Tarot*, Thorsons, 1991

Altman, Nathaniel, *Discover Palmistry*, Aquarian, 1991

Anderton, Bill, *Life Cycles*, Foulsham, 1990

Anderton, Bill, *Meditation For Every Day*, Piatkus, 1995

Angelo, Jack, *Your Healing Power*, Piatkus, 1994

Arcarti, Kristyna, *I Ching For Beginners*, Hodder & Stoughton, 1994

Arcarti, Kristyna, *Palmistry For Beginners*, Hodder & Stoughton, 1993

Bailey, Arthur, *Dowsing For Health*, Foulsham, 1990

Chetwynd, Tom, *Dictionary For Dreamers*, Aquarian, 1993

Chetwynd, Tom, *Dictionary Of Symbols*, Aquarian, 1993

Crawford, E.A. & Kennedy, T., *Chinese Elemental Astrology*, Piatkus, 1990

Cunningham, Scott, *Art Of Divination*, Crossing Press, 1993

Cunningham, Scott, *Sacred Sleep*, Crossing Press, 1992

Dee, Nerys, *Understanding Dreams*, Thorsons, 1991

Furlong, David, *Complete Healer*, Piatkus, 1995

Garen, Nancy, *Tarot Made Easy*, Piatkus, 1990

Gawain, Shakti, *Creative Visualization*, Bantam, 1982

Geddes, Sheila, *Art Of Astrology*, Aquarian, 1982

Graves, Tom, *Elements Of Pendulum Dowsing*, Element, 1991

Hewitt, James, *Complete Relaxation Book*, Rider, 1982

Holzer, Hans, *Psychic Side of Dreams*, Llewellyn, 1992

Jung, Carl (ed.), *Man And His Symbols*, Pan, 1978

King, Bernard, *Elements Of The Runes*, Element, 1993

Linn, Denise, *Past Lives, Present Dreams*, Piatkus, 1995

Mann, A.T., *Millennium Prophecies*, Element, 1993

Mayo, Jeff, *Teach Yourself Astrology*, Hodder & Stoughton, 1992

Nielsen, Greg & Polansky, Joseph, *Pendulum Power*, Aquarian, 1986

Northage, Ivy, *Mediumship Made Simple*, College of Psychic Studies, London, 1994

Oracle Of Mlle Lenormand, Urania Verlags AG, Switzerland, 1989

Ostrom, Joseph, *Understanding Auras*, Aquarian, 1993

Pennick, Nigel, *Runic Astrology*, Capall Bann, 1995

Sneddon, Paul, *Self-Development With The I Ching*, Foulsham, 1990

Stewart, R.J., *Elements of Prophecy*, Element Books, 1990

Summers, Catherine & Vayne, Julian, *Self-Development With The Tarot*, Foulsham, 1992

Thorpe, Charles, *Card Fortune-Telling*, Foulsham, 1989

Trevelyan, George, *A Vision Of The Aquarian Age*, Gateway, 1994

Tzu, Lao, *Tao Te Ching*, Penguin, 1963

Vaughan, Richard, *Numbers As Symbols For Self-Discovery*, CRCS, 1985

Wilhelm, Richard (tr.), *I Ching Or Book Of Changes*, Penguin, 1989

Index